Unconventional Business

Five Keys to Growing a Business God's Way

by

Rick Boxx

D0833515

Unconventional Business

Rick Boxx

Integrity Resource Center
PO Box 25301
Overland Park, KS 66225
913.782.9333

Unless otherwise noted, "Scripture quotations taken from the New American Standard Bible®, Copyright © 1960, 1962, 1963, 1968, 1971, 1972, 1973, 1975, 1977, 1995 by The Lockman Foundation. Used by permission." (www.Lockman.org).

This book is manufactured in the United States of America.

Library of Congress Cataloging in Publication Data in Progress.

CONTENTS

INTRODUCTION

Business leaders are constantly looking for solutions to their problems. Many are like lemmings, unfortunately, jumping off the cliff to follow the latest business fad. They jump from one trend to another, hoping to find long-term answers to profitability.

For those who truly desire a long-term consistent strategy, there is a guide that has been used for thousands of years. Although it has passed the test throughout every business cycle, to the world, it's an unconventional business strategy.

The Bible has answers for life's issues, but few have ever considered it as a tool to help them in their business life. If you've never read the Bible through the lens of a business leader instead of as a spouse or parent, you likely have missed the amazing wisdom buried in it.

This book is designed to be a practical guide for your business. It addresses biblical approaches to planning, finances, human resource challenges, and more, but it takes courage. God's ways are not our ways. If you've ever spent much time in the Bible, you have probably recognized that it is full of paradoxes. When the world tells you to pay yourself first, God's Word teaches us to give the first of our profits to his work.

When the world tells us to use other people's money and leverage your business to get a higher return, God says to trust him for your funding instead of your banker. To implement God's strategies will take courage, but it also will pay great dividends. You will have God leading you into wisdom only he can provide. He will bless you with eternal rewards and a feeling of significance that will pale in comparison to amassing wealth that has no meaning.

In Romans 12:2, the Apostle Paul teaches: "And do not be conformed to this world, but be transformed by the renewing of your mind, so that you may prove what the will of God is, that which is good and acceptable and perfect."

My challenge to you is that you will keep this book as a resource, and not regard it as a book you read and discard. This book is a tool to come back to over and over. Use it to transform your thinking about business and to refresh your memory of God's calling on your life and how to carry out that calling in a way that pleases God.

May God bless you, your family, and your business!

Rick Boxx
Founder and CEO
Integrity Resource Center
www.integrityresource.org

ACKNOWLEDGEMENTS

Although this book project began as a rewrite of a previous book, it became obvious to me very quickly that God wanted this to become a much more comprehensive look at his Word and how it might be used to help business leaders practically apply scripture to all areas of their business. A project like this cannot be done in a vacuum by one person.

Instead, it takes a team of people. I am grateful for the great people God has surrounded me with as I've developed this new manuscript. I am thankful for my editor, Susan Tolleson of Propel Book Coaching, my graphic designer, Tom Avery, the *Integrity Resource Center* team, including: Kip Blue, Cecil Carder, Cindy Parsons, Leslie Hull, Laura Jeffries, David Alexander, and Steve Darr.

Most of all, I'm grateful for my wife, Kathy, and my children—Megan, Jeremy, and Rebekah—who were patient with me every Saturday morning while I worked on this book rather than spending time with them.

Finally, all wisdom, talents, and skills I have come from my heavenly Father. I am so grateful that God saved me from my disastrous path and that he not only gave me meaning and purpose, but answered my prayer of allowing me to serve him through business—something I have been passionate about since I was a child.

First Key:

Developing a
God-centered Plan

CHAPTER ONE

Nehemiah's Seven-step Plan

"The plans of the diligent lead surely to advantage,
but everyone who is hasty comes surely to poverty."
Proverbs 21:5

For more than 140 years, Jerusalem had been lying in ruins. Many had tried to rebuild it without success. The few people who lived in this holy city had grown accustomed to stepping over the rubble, with little vision that anything would ever change.

That is, until Nehemiah discovered God's plan for his future work. Nehemiah was a cupbearer for the king in Persia. He had likely never seen Jerusalem, yet he was an Israelite with a deep passion for his people's homeland.

After Nehemiah had an encounter with his brother and learned of the sad disrepair of Jerusalem, his world changed. And so did Jerusalem. Following God's divine plan, this great leader directed his people in both a spiritual revival and a miraculous rebuilding of the walls around Jerusalem.

The result of Nehemiah's work was success beyond anyone's imagination! In Nehemiah 6:15–16 we read, "So the wall was completed on the twenty-fifth of the month Elul, in fifty-two days. When all our enemies heard of it, and all the nations surrounding us saw it, they lost their confidence; for they recognized that this work had been accomplished with the help of our God."

Wouldn't you like that kind of help for your business? With God's help, Nehemiah succeeded where others had failed. Imagine what God may be able to do with your business if you seek and follow his plan. If you have never taken the time to explore the book of Nehemiah, I encourage you to read through it as I introduce you to seven steps Nehemiah took to develop and implement his plan for Jerusalem's restoration.

When I started a consulting practice in 1995, I surveyed many business owners about planning. Not surprisingly, when I asked them if planning was important, nearly 100 percent confirmed the importance of having a business plan. But when I asked how many had done any form of business planning in the last two years, less than half of these same entrepreneurs responded affirmatively.

If planning is important—the Bible even acknowledges its importance—then why don't more business owners plan? Effective planning requires knowledge of a process that works, and few entrepreneurs have this knowledge or skill set. In this chapter, I'm going to introduce you to a God-inspired planning model that worked for Nehemiah.

Nehemiah's Planning Model

In 1995 the Lord opened my eyes to a startling discovery: the book of Nehemiah. This biblical text is a great model for how to fulfill a God-sized vision through planning and implementation. In fact, this biblical blueprint is so powerfully effective that we developed *Integrity Resource Center's* "Foundation Plan" to assist businesses in proper planning and ongoing implementation. Let's look at the steps Nehemiah used to accomplish an incredible feat—rebuilding the wall in record time, and rebuilding the spiritual fabric of his people.

A close examination of Nehemiah's journey helped me to develop the following seven steps for planning:

Step 1: Pray fervently
Step 2: Assess thoroughly
Step 3: Seek God's vision
Step 4: Develop strategies and tactics
Step 5: Count the cost

Step 6: Implement the plan

Step 7: Follow up and be accountable

Step 1: Pray fervently

Throughout the book of Nehemiah, you will find the cornerstone of Nehemiah's activity was prayer. Nehemiah was dedicated to prayer, but even more so, to waiting on God's timing to answer those prayers.

His story begins with his discovery about the disrepair of Jerusalem. As an Israelite who was passionate for his heritage and people, he was greatly grieved by what he heard about Jerusalem. Many entrepreneurs might have taken that information, climbed on their camel and headed for the homeland to fix the problem. Others might have said, "That's terrible," and then gone about their business. Not Nehemiah. He began to pray. And pray. And pray.

Nehemiah prayed for a remarkable four months about this burden. Finally, the time was right. The Lord showed him favor in the eyes of the king. The timing was so right that Nehemiah not only got permission to leave his important role as cupbearer to go rebuild the wall, but he received the king's blessing, all of the necessary provisions to rebuild the wall, all of the necessary authority to do the job, and all of the necessary provisions to feed himself and his staff.

The king was abundantly generous with Nehemiah and granted all of his requests. This didn't come from Nehemiah's skill and strength, but from God's. Nehemiah's earnest and patient prayers led him to the proper time and approach.

Business leaders, if you want an effective plan for your business, don't miss this most important step. Pray! Pray for God's purpose, pray that you clearly understand his purpose, and that God will use you in an effective way to accomplish his purpose.

Throughout the entire planning process in your business, pray at every turn. Pray, and then patiently wait for God's timing and leading, not yours. In our society, waiting at a drive-up window longer than three minutes seems unbearable. The hardest thing for most of us to do is to wait on God's timing.

At *Integrity Resource Center* (IRC), we provide phone counsel to many business leaders. Occasionally we are blessed to hear the end result of our counsel. One day a woman called to give me an update on her husband, a pastor who eventually went into business for himself. According to his wife, the business was struggling, the family was suffering, but most concerning to her was that her husband had stopped praying or seeking the Lord's guidance. Our team member prayed with this troubled woman specifically that God would help her husband to see the importance of turning back to him.

The reason for her update was a praise report. Less than an hour after our prayer, a customer told her husband that God wanted him to know that if he wanted his business to succeed, he better get back on his knees and seek God. If this wasn't enough, the very next day someone else approached him at church, telling him they felt like they had been instructed to encourage him to turn back to God.

This former pastor got the message. He rekindled his relationship with God, and the last report was that his business was prospering. A simple prayer started the action necessary to bring another one of God's children closer to him.

Step 2: Assess thoroughly

When Nehemiah first arrived in Jerusalem, he knew work couldn't begin on the wall until he assessed Jerusalem's current situation. After examining its state of affairs for three days, he went out in the evening with fresh perspective and inspected the wall.

The local people had lived with Jerusalem's disrepair for so long that the heartbreak had become complacency. It took an objective look from an outsider like Nehemiah to determine the magnitude of the problem. Just

> *The key areas to examine in most businesses are financial, operational, sales and marketing, and management. For nonprofits, fundraising and promotion may be substituted for sales and marketing.*

like the wall and the people in Nehemiah's day, many businesses today are broken, both spiritually and financially. They need an objective assessment.

The first phase of *IRC*'s "Foundation Plan" is a diagnostic assessment, an objective opinion about your strengths and weaknesses. Although Nehemiah had different issues to address, the principle remains consistent—assess your key areas. The key areas to examine in most businesses are financial, operational, sales and marketing, and management. For nonprofits, fundraising and promotion may be substituted for sales and marketing.

Financial

By looking at a business' past financial trends and its current financial condition objectively, it becomes easier to determine what strengths should be emphasized and what weaknesses need to be overcome. We will review key financial factors in Chapter 11 that cover the most important issues in almost any business.

If you are not financially oriented, you should probably seek outside counsel to give you an objective view. Sometimes, even if you are financially oriented, you may be too close to the situation to be objective.

Operational

Producing your service or product requires many day-to-day operational activities to take place. If all of these activities are not handled properly, your customer suffers, which means your business will eventually suffer. Quality and productivity are probably two of the most difficult—but important—factors to review in the operational side of any business. They are both subjective in nature and really boil down to perception, sometimes even more than reality. A survey is probably the most effective tool for assessing quality and productivity.

Discussing your strengths and weaknesses and surveying your staff and customers will help you to determine your operational shortcomings. Summarizing these results is the first step in recognizing the problems that need to be addressed.

Sales and marketing

If you are in a for-profit business, revenue drives your business. Without sales, you have no reason to exist. If you have the right price on your product or service, but not enough volume, you will fail. It is just as dangerous to have the right amount of volume, but the wrong price. If your price is too low, you will go broke in a hurry.

Pricing, **promotion**, **product**, and **positioning** are commonly referred to as the **four Ps of marketing**. Promotion includes many aspects of selling, while the other items primarily address marketing issues. Each of these areas should have an underlying principle or strategy driving your approach. If not, it is likely you are reactively addressing issues, rather than building a long-term marketing strategy.

As part of your assessment phase, you should objectively assess how well your organization's sales and marketing efforts are aligned with its vision and mission.

Management

When assessing management, you are typically looking at how people, money, or time are managed. We have already dealt with money, so that leaves time and people. Managing time requires a close look at the purposes of both the company and individuals. Time is generally wasted on urgent issues that are not really important to your long-term goals and purposes. In terms of people, examine employee turnover, trends in productivity and quality, and how close the company and individuals are to meeting goals.

In order to determine management's effectiveness, you really need to get unbiased feedback from your employees about the people and the systems being used to manage. You also need to examine results—as compared to expectations—of employees and the management team. This can be done with surveys, observation, asking questions, and reviewing tangible data.

Step 3: Seek God's vision

It is easy to miss the big picture in the book of Nehemiah. Although the book spends a great deal of time on rebuilding the wall, it is obvious from Nehemiah's prayer that both he and God were interested in restoring the people spiritually, as well as rebuilding the wall.

For a practical plan to be implemented, it requires a clear vision, mission, and core values. Nehemiah knew the vision and purpose was to turn the hearts of the Israelites back to God and restore them to their rightful home. It's clear that Nehemiah modeled and encouraged faith and integrity. These core values guided his decisions.

Determine God's vision for your business

As a business owner, you have probably heard about vision, mission, and core value statements. You may even have told yourself, "This is just another fad exercise for businesses that wastes time." However, if done with the proper perspective and implementation, this exercise could save your business thousands of dollars. Poor strategic decisions can be avoided when tested against these clearly defined statements of organizational purpose and intent.

Let me give you an example. We once worked with a prepress company that was at a pivotal stage in their business. Strategically they knew it was critical for them to diversify into digital printing in order to survive. This was a costly decision that caused them to borrow a great deal of money and crippled their cash flow, but the large short-term investment was already beginning to pay dividends.

At this crucial point in their business, the two owners were in the process of working with *IRC* to develop their vision when they informed me they had been seriously researching purchasing a doughnut franchise. After drawing out of them their true passions, and adding clarity to their focus, they realized the absurdity of buying a doughnut franchise when they were called to focus on their customer's printing and prepress needs. This near tactical mistake would have likely cost them thousands of dollars, and been the final blow to their business.

Vision comes from God. Throughout the Bible, you see God proactively coming to his chosen leaders with a vision. For Abraham, it was: "Go to the land I will show you and I will make you a great nation." For Moses, it was to lead the Israelites out of Egypt and into the Promised Land. For others, like Nehemiah, the vision was placed as a burden on his heart, which was confirmed by prayer and circumstances. The king's willingness, as a result of Nehemiah's prayer, assured him he was doing God's will.

As Henry Blackaby points out in *Experiencing God,* God is not in the business of developing a plan for us individually, and then shaping the world around us, as much as many of us like to think. Instead, he has a vision for his people, and expects us to join in and play the role he has chosen for us. But if we choose not to join him in his work, rest assured he will still accomplish his plan, with or without us.

If we are business leaders sold out for God, we should recognize that our businesses are God's to be used to accomplish **his** vision. This requires that we seek out his vision, and keep it very clear to the people around us so that we can effectively achieve his purposes.

Amos 3:7 teaches, "Surely the Sovereign Lord does nothing without revealing his plan to his servants the prophets." God wants us to know what he is about. I have seen many occasions when God places a very similar vision on several leaders' hearts at the same time. This is incredible affirmation that God is at work, and should not be overlooked or viewed as competition. If God has put a vision in or a passion on our hearts, we need to examine it closely, pray about it, seek affirmation, and then determine what role God is calling us to play in that vision.

Nehemiah had a clear calling and a passion. He knew God wanted him to rebuild the wall of Jerusalem. Yet, when Nehemiah carried out God's purposes, a remarkable thing happened; a spiritual revival occurred. Don't presume that what God has called you to do has no eternal significance; just determine his vision and be faithful, and the rest will work out.

Assemble the pieces. In order to assist in the vision-creation process, let me introduce some questions to consider. The answers to these questions will provide phrases, words, or concepts, which can be refined into the vision statement itself. Write your thoughts to the following questions.

1. What do you see God doing around you?
2. What things of eternal significance do you believe God could accomplish through your business?
3. If you were able to observe your eulogy thirty to forty years from now, what would you hope your vendors, customers, suppliers, and employees would say about your company and your accomplishments?
4. When you stand before God upon your death, and he asks you what you accomplished with the business he blessed you with, what would you like to say?
5. What **could** your business be better at than anyone else in the world?

After answering these questions, draft your first attempt at a brief vision statement. You can refine it later.

Develop a mission statement

Jane had a successful sod farm when a truck salesman convinced her to partner with him in a used truck business. She put up the money and handled the administrative affairs; he sold trucks. From the beginning, their mission was truck sales, with used parts and truck modifications as their secondary focus. Sales skyrocketed, profits were good, and they won awards for their fast growth. They were on top of the world.

But just as quickly, things fell apart. When Jane found out the salesman was involved in some illegal activities, she quickly bought him out and terminated all of his relatives. Now

Jane was forced to determine how to run a truck business that she knew very little about.

Over the next two years, as profits turned to significant losses, the business shifted its focus from selling trucks to buying salvage parts. They lost sight of their original mission. Their original mission had proven successful, but their change of direction towards salvage parts proved disastrous. In very short order, this sizable business dismantled and failed.

This is a dramatic example of what can happen when your mission is not clear, or it gets changed without careful consideration of the customer's needs and desires.

A mission statement should describe what the organization does, why it exists, and whom it serves. It should be simple, concise, and direct. A paragraph or less is preferred. It should be long enough to explain the mission, but short enough for staff to remember.

Since the mission will need to be carried out by all parties involved in the business, it is helpful to have the staff's buy in and input. Soliciting their ideas on key words or phrases to be included adds value to the process. There were many leaders involved in the process of rebuilding the wall of Jerusalem. They could have tried to muscle in on Nehemiah's role, but their mission was clear—to build their section of the wall. The mission statement should help a worker determine for what portion of the vision **they** are responsible.

The right questions help craft the statement. Answering the following questions will help you develop the right mission statement for your organization.

1. How can God use your business to fulfill his vision?
2. Describe what your organization does, and what it should be doing to achieve the vision.
3. Why does your business exist?

4. Who does your business serve? This may include customers, shareholders, employees, and God.

Create core values

LRN Consulting's international survey discovered that businesses that create a culture based on values rather than dogmatic rules and policies far outperform their peers. Established values consistently applied by a company help all parties involved know what is expected. As shepherds over the flock of employees God has entrusted to us, it is necessary that we focus our staff on the values that will best enable them to carry out the mission.

If you develop a set of core values that are regularly emphasized throughout your business, your staff will have a better understanding of what you consider most important. You also will have communicated to them that their job may be contingent upon them holding to the same values while they represent your organization.

In developing core values, you may find it helpful to review and consider the following:

- the "golden rule" (Matt. 7:12)
- the Ten Commandments (Ex. 20)
- Leviticus 19
- values you personally try to maintain and hold as valuable
- values critical to the success of your business.

Take a moment to jot down words or phrases you hold as values to be considered. After the list is developed, try to cull down the list to four or five key values. The values statement will lose its impact if too many are included.

Step 4: Develop strategy and tactics

The balanced approach Nehemiah exhibited is very impressive. He was prayerful, patient, and a visionary, but when he had planned appropriately, he became a man of action. He was so focused on his task that even though his adversaries tried countless times, they couldn't pull him away from his duties. There are many people of action, but who often don't plan. Or someone is a planner who never pulls the trigger. Nehemiah gave us an ideal model for both.

After a plan has a clear vision, it's time to develop a strategy to accomplish the vision. Nehemiah brilliantly broke the project down into forty-one sections of wall with specific teams rebuilding each section. Your strategy can make or break your business, so take the time to think through the different options, and when possible, test the strategy on a small scale first to assure it's the right approach.

After you've developed your strategy, you still need to implement it. That requires big-picture ideas to be broken down into detailed tactics. Without detailed tactics or action plans, it is unlikely you will achieve your goals. Consider using the **SMART method** to assure that they are:

> **S**pecific
> **M**easurable
> **A**ttainable
> **R**ealistic
> **T**ime restricted

It's really as simple as thinking through the individual steps you are going to take, setting yourself a deadline, writing it on your calendar, and having someone hold you accountable. If you learn to do this consistently, you will be amazed at how much you can accomplish.

Step 5: Count the cost

Just when everything seems to be going according to plan, suddenly money problems can rear their ugly head. Nehemiah was no exception. It appeared that everyone was working together in teams to complete the wall in record-breaking time, when out of the blue, the people begin complaining about their poverty.

This was not just a small money problem. Apparently there was a famine, combined with a large debt, excessive taxes, and lenders that were less than kind. This serious problem required Nehemiah to call a time-out on the important work of rebuilding the wall. He had to stop and referee between the lenders and the borrowers. He also had to consider how this was affecting his work. In other words, just like Jesus recommended, he had to count the cost before going forward. The workers could not do their duties well if they were hungry and in bondage. Don't you wish you could call a Nehemiah in to convince your lenders to cancel your debts and pay you back the interest?

In business, we need to count the cost of the plans we desire to implement. Plans for serious expansion may not be feasible if the business is already strangled with debt. Just like for Nehemiah, a plan to get out of bondage needs to be developed before going forward. You need to ask yourself hard questions like: How will you fund future costs? Will you use debt or equity?

For success to happen, this also requires a budget of what the future needs to look like financially. Prudently look ahead and develop a realistic budget that reflects how you are going to go about accomplishing your plans. After it's done, ask yourself how you will fund future costs. Can your budget survive the hard times?

Without a clear understanding of the financial aspects of your business, you cannot succeed long term. It's critical that finances become a priority in your plan for the future.

Step 6: Implement the plan

As I develop plans with business owners, one of the most difficult and frustrating aspects is seeing that the plan actually gets implemented. Nehemiah knew how to implement. After he mapped out his plan and set his goals, he called together important leaders in the community, sold his vision, allocated the work, and started the project.

Nehemiah was extremely focused and kept working in spite of adversities. The Bible tells us that even when important rulers called for him to meet with them, he said no. When he feared being attacked, his people were armed with weapons in one hand and continued their work with the other hand. What perseverance!

Once you have your plan for your business, be like Nehemiah. Get focused, stay on track, and keep working the plan. Nehemiah led by example, but he also was wise enough to know when he needed help, so he rallied the existing leaders to develop their own teams to do their section of the work. He did have to pause and assess their progress and adjust problem areas at times, but he never forgot what they were to accomplish.

If you have trouble implementing, look for someone to hold you accountable. Set specific checkpoints to review your progress with another person who cares enough to hold you to your goals and deadlines.

Step 7: Follow-up and be accountable

Nehemiah could have quit after the wall was completed. He could have gone back home victorious, bragging about his accomplishment of building the wall in a record fifty-two days. The world tells us to quit while you're ahead. However, Nehemiah knew that God was not finished with all that he had in mind for Jerusalem.

Nehemiah knew that for a plan to be fruitful, a follow-up strategy needed to be developed and implemented. Many people develop a plan for the next year and then stop. What about the following year? Isn't there more to do? Doesn't God have more in store for your business to accomplish than next year's goals?

After Nehemiah finished the wall, he was open for God's leading as to what was next. He knew that God's plan was not about a wall, but about lives. He researched what had happened to all of the Israelites who should have been living in Jerusalem, and worked to bring them back to the city.

After the people were assembled, a great revival broke out as they were convicted by the word of God. Eventually, Nehemiah did have to go back to the king. He wanted assurance that his plan would continue while he was away, so he chose wise, Godly leaders to manage the work. Even with this kind of preparation, the best plans can go bad without some accountability.

When Nehemiah came back, he was furious to find that all of the sinful activities had resumed. There was no respect for the Sabbath again, and even some of the Levites had allowed their family to marry neighboring peoples.

I have learned many lessons from these passages in Nehemiah. A plan is never complete. It needs to be an ongoing process that is constantly monitored and modified. For a plan to be effective, there needs to be both wise leaders and accountability. The plan needs to be focused on both the eternal and material results. If you only look for the material harvest and set your goals accordingly, you will miss God's purpose, which is generally about relationships.

Summary

The book of Nehemiah is a great model for planning the future of your business. The lessons are new and fresh each time I study this insightful book. The seven steps of this amazing leader are as follows:

1. **Pray fervently**—Seek the Lord and his plan, and it will be revealed.
2. **Assess thoroughly**—Look for the strengths and weaknesses in your business; assess the damage.
3. **Seek God's vision**—Identify God's vision, mission, and values.
4. **Develop the strategy and tactics**—Determine the most effective strategy and break it down into tactical steps.
5. **Count the cost**—Develop a budget that is reasonable and stick to it.
6. **Implement the plan**—Take action and implement the plan; a plan on a shelf doesn't do any good.
7. **Follow-up and be accountable**—Planning is an ongoing process that requires constant follow-up and accountability.

Over the years, we have guided many businesses using Nehemiah's planning process. We've seen them experience great return on their investment of time and money, and even greater investment in the things that matter to God. If you truly desire to build a business God's way, visit our website at *www.integrityresource.org* to schedule a time with us to seek God's vision for your business.

CHAPTER TWO

Developing a Ministry Plan

"Set your minds on things above, not on earthly things."
Colossians 3:2

In 1970, world-famous economist Milton Friedman, who later accepted the Nobel Prize in Economics, declared that the only purpose of business is profit. Since many believed Friedman to be the most influential economist of the twentieth century, it wasn't long before businesses wholeheartedly embraced Friedman's singular focus on shareholder value, and discarded any notion of social responsibility or generosity to their communities.

This focus increased the profitability and shareholder value of many of the largest corporations, but it seemed to strip them of any sign of a soul or conscience. Greed became the mantra of corporate America, climaxing in a 1987 film called "Wall Street" where actor Michael Douglas proclaimed that "greed is good." Soon thereafter, the moral fabric of corporate America significantly unraveled.

In his letter to the Colossians, the apostle Paul urged them as new followers of Christ to give up their sinful motives, including greed, and to set their minds on things above. In Colossians 3:17, he went on to proclaim, "Whatever you do, whether in word or deed, do it all in the name of the Lord Jesus, giving thanks to God the Father through him." As followers of Jesus, bringing glory to God is *our* purpose, even when we are leading a business. Profit is a necessary by-product of glorifying God, not the other way around.

If God has blessed us with the responsibility of leading a business, he desires us to have a much broader view of our stewardship responsibility than just making money. Developing a ministry plan for your business is an ideal way to proactively consider how God might choose to use your organization to advance his kingdom while caring for the needs of your team and their families.

The five elements of a ministry plan

In any organization, there will be time when your people have personal needs that can get in the way of the work. If you become too focused on tasks or motivated by profit, you may be tempted to ignore or even cast aside those who slow down your project due to their personal challenges.

Nehemiah had to confront this kind of issue after a famine devastated his workers. He wanted to get his project completed, yet he knew that his higher priority was to take care of the needs of the people. He listened carefully and then developed a plan to minister to these people. His plan resulted in relief for his workers that freed them up emotionally and financially. This enabled them to get back to work, and likely built trust between Nehemiah and his team.

If glorifying God is our primary purpose in business, then it makes sense to start with what Jesus called the two greatest commandments. In Matthew 22, Jesus was asked what he believed to be the greatest commandment. He responded, "Love the Lord your God with all your heart and with all your soul and with all your mind. This is the first and greatest commandment. And the second is like it: Love your neighbor as yourself. All the Law and the Prophets hang on these two commandments."

Out of these two commandments, we can build the framework for a ministry plan. The first two elements are tied to the first commandment of loving God. The remaining three elements come from the second commandment of loving others.

As you develop your ministry plan, consider the following five elements:

1. Evangelism
2. Discipleship
3. Loving your team
4. Loving customers, suppliers and competitors
5. Loving your community

Business leaders typically recognize the value of having a business plan. They will work through a strategic plan and may also have a marketing plan, but very few have ever considered developing a *ministry* plan for their business.

> *A ministry plan focuses you on how you can have eternal significance on and through your business.*

Like any plan, a ministry plan can help you become purposeful about developing goals and action plans for the future of your business. The kinds of goals, however, are uniquely different. A ministry plan focuses you on how you can have eternal significance in and through your business.

This concept of a ministry plan may make you uncomfortable. It certainly is not for the faint hearted. A ministry plan requires leaving our comfort zone, and it comes with risks. However, the rewards are eternal and significant. Incredible things can and do happen when God's people open their workplace to his work.

A ministry plan should begin with an *objective*: What do you hope to accomplish? It doesn't have to be anything fancy. Just succinctly and plainly state your desired outcome of performing ministry through your business. This will allow you to remain focused on the important eternal tasks for which you have been called.

After your objective has been stated, you need to dig into the meat of the plan. Your plan should concentrate on the five key areas addressed above. In each section of your plan, outline your purpose for focusing on this activity, and the acceptable and unacceptable methods to accomplish your goals.

Evangelism

In Matthew 28:19, Jesus told his disciples, "Therefore go and make disciples of all nations, baptizing them in the name of the Father and of the Son and of the Holy Spirit." This was one of Jesus' last instructions. It was the essence of his mission to not only *be* the sacrifice that would atone for our sins, but also to begin the process of spreading the good news of the gospel. This is a charge for each and every believer in Jesus that is applicable today as much as it was back then.

The workplace is ripe for the harvest, but as in Jesus' time, the workers are few. As business leaders, we have a tremendous opportunity to share the gospel with people who may never enter a place of worship. Unfortunately, this platform is seriously underused. Too many Christians are quick to appoint their pastor as the one who should save souls.

Jesus could have appointed and anointed the clergy of the day to build the church and to preach the gospel. Instead, he told a bunch of fishermen, a tax collector, and other assorted people of commerce to go forth and do it. We need to recognize our call, be obedient to that call, and quit hiding behind our rationalizations for avoiding this difficult—but very exciting—possibility.

In developing a ministry plan for your business, leadership needs to determine what policies and practices should be addressed in order to guide your team. Even in your zealousness to be evangelistic, you'll need to be respectful of each person in the workplace. A friend once had an employee who had a tendency to evangelize to brand-new employees before he had built any kind of relationship with them. My friend had to reign in this "hyper evangelist," which led to the need for a policy outlining how all team members should be treated with respect and dignity.

When God is leading, you never have to worry about the method you use to save the lost, but it is beneficial to be prepared to give a reason for the faith that is within you. To assist you, I asked Mark Lockard, a friend and former business owner who has had great success with evangelism in his workplace, to share some pointers on how to effectively present the gospel to employees and in the marketplace.

1. **Know your own story**. Be prepared to tell your story of salvation quickly and effectively.

2. **Pray for opportunities**. Pray that God would give you soul-winning eyes that do not overlook opportunities.

3. **Stay in a close intimate relationship with him**. Experience God's glory yourself. People can't catch what you don't have.

4. **Respond out of relationship**. God draws people to himself. Our job is to recognize whom God is drawing, and be ready and willing to respond.

5. **Develop relationships by sharing God's love**. Look for opportunities to share God's love to a lost and hurting world. Listen to others, and take time to go out of your way for them.

6. **Have a plan**. Know the method or tools you are going to use when God presents you with an opportunity. Be sensitive and flexible in your method, and make sure the method doesn't get in the way. Relate the gospel to their specific need.

7. **Be purposeful and intentional**. Make appointments, and invite others to lunch or dinner, church, etc. Look for ways to spend time with them to earn the right to

share Christ. Pray that God would enable you to live an upright life.

Evangelism can be tough enough without confusing the matter further with workplace issues. Running a profitable business while responding to opportunities that come up to share the gospel with others can be trying. The issue of employer/employee relations can further complicate things. Many employees will feel that you expect them to submit to your ideas as their employer. Salvation doesn't come through coercion. God designed it to be a willing choice. Be sensitive to their concerns.

You also need to be sensitive to legal issues that come with workplace evangelism. In their booklet "Christian Rights in the Workplace," the American Center for Law and Justice states: "An employer can talk about his religious beliefs with employees as long as employees know that continued employment or advancement within the company is not conditioned upon acquiescence in the employer's religious beliefs.... Employers must be careful, however, not to persist in witnessing if the employee objects. Such unwanted proselytizing could be deemed religious harassment."

Discipleship

A good shepherd makes sure that his flock has its needs met, both spiritually and physically. A portion of your ministry plan should address your employees' need for spiritual growth. If you have brand-new believers, they naturally need to be discipled and steered towards a strong relationship with the Lord. Existing believers also need to be continually challenged in growing in their relationship with the Lord, and in applying God's truth to their daily environment.

Discipleship can take place in a one-on-one situation or in a group setting. Many businesses have voluntary Bible study groups meeting in their office before or after work hours, or during break times. This can be an easy way to encourage employees to go deeper into the Word, and to hear more from you about the beliefs you value and how they can be applied in the workplace. Just be sure employees recognize that the activity is voluntary and that it is being held outside of work hours.

In your ministry plan, address the methodologies you are willing to use, and what is not acceptable, so that your boundaries are well defined. Encourage other believers in your workplace to disciple, as well. The real fruit comes when you are able to have more than one person in the workplace actively practicing and teaching God's Word.

Loving your team

Ministering to the needs of your employees goes hand in hand with evangelism and discipleship. Paul teaches in 1 Timothy 5:8: "If anyone does not provide for his relatives, and especially for his immediate family, he has denied the faith and is worse than an unbeliever." The principle behind this passage is that we are to take care of our own. For a business leader, this means God has placed people in your care for a reason, and they should be treated as your "business family."

People have needs that are emotional, physical, psychological, and spiritual. If you ignore these needs, not only will you damage your opportunity to evangelize and disciple these people, but you will be shirking your responsibility as the steward over these people. Jesus' most effective ministry came from his willingness to meet the individual needs of people, both physically and spiritually.

There are many different ways to minister to your employees, but the most important way is to be available and sensitive to listening when they have issues they feel need to be addressed. One method I've seen used effectively is to set up an employee assistance fund. These funds can be designed to help staff with needs. Maybe an employee is about to have their utilities shut off, or their home foreclosed on, or they're drowning from medical bills. These are opportunities to show the love of Christ by having either the company or other employees—or preferably both—pitch in to help in an employee's time of need.

Marketplace Chaplains has a program that many companies use to provide an outlet for their employees. These chaplains help employees with family tragedies, weddings, funerals, addictions, and many other issues important to them. This can be a non-threatening way for an employer to provide spiritual counsel for an employee without the employee feeling job pressure.

Be creative in finding ways to meet the ongoing needs of your staff. They will appreciate it, and it will likely bear eternal rewards.

Loving customers, suppliers, and competitors

Businesses have tremendous influence in their community. They make daily contact with customers, suppliers, civic organizations, politicians, and many public servants. These are all opportunities to make disciples for Jesus Christ. Demonstrating excellence in all that you do, loving others, and serving people can change the very nature of your city.

A pastor recently shared with me a story about a group of business owners who came together to talk about using their businesses to God's glory. The pastor challenged them to begin praying for their competition. Rather than view them as an enemy, he challenged these men to love them. The next week one of these men did just that.

It seems this man had been so convicted by that conversation that he went home and called his competitor. He apologized for the times he had degraded him to prospective customers. He went a step further and said his company would no longer say derogatory things about the competition, and would actually begin referring customers to them when they were a more suitable solution. The very next day, both parties referred customers to each other, and began working towards making their industry and businesses more cooperative and stronger.

Is God calling you to consider in your ministry plan how you can better serve others? Whether it is your competition, customers, suppliers, or other business people, look for ways to shine the light of Christ into the lives of others. Solicit input from your staff as to how you can better accomplish this noble goal.

Loving your community

Employees have needs, but so do people in your community. In Leviticus 19:9-10, God commanded the Israelites, "When you reap the harvest of your land, do not reap to the very edges of your field or gather the gleanings of your harvest. Do not go over your vineyard a second time or pick up the grapes that have fallen. Leave them for the poor and the alien. I am the Lord your God."

God desires us to use the excess in our business to help the poor, aliens (unbelievers), and widows and orphans. (See James 1:27.) We need to be obedient to this standard by using our business resources to assist with the needs of the community. Businesses have the unique opportunity for their people and time to be very effective. Unfortunately, we see large Fortune 500 businesses leveraging this strength for activities that do not always glorify God, while many smaller businesses that have a heart for God's work overlook this creative way to assist the community for God's glory.

Look for activities in which your business could assist that would meet the needs of oppressed people. For example, single parents really need support in today's world. They are similar to the widows of biblical times. They have limited resources and big responsibilities without very much help. God would be pleased to see us use our time, talent, and money to help these hurting and stressed out people in our community.

Summary

A ministry plan can be a scary thought. It takes a large leap of faith. It also requires that your faith become real—not only to you—but also to the staff around you. If you properly outline your goals and objectives, communicate them to your staff, and then model them. I think you will be amazed at how God will honor your efforts. The harvest is ripe, but the workers are few. Are you up for the challenge?

Second Key:

Prepare Yourself

as a Leader

CHAPTER THREE
Ordering Your Priorities

"But seek first His kingdom and His righteousness, and all these
things will be added to you. So do not worry about tomorrow; for
tomorrow will care for itself."
Matthew 6:33–34

It was 1955. Stanley Tam, the founder of U.S. Plastic Corporation, had a decision to make. While speaking at an evangelistic crusade, he had been praying fervently for the lost souls of Columbia when God gave him a challenge. What he heard was, "Stanley, if you agree that a soul has the greatest value in the whole world and is the only investment you can make in this life that will pay dividends throughout eternity, would you be willing to go back to Ohio and become an employee of mine?"

Stanley knew that God was asking him to donate the remainder of his ownership in U.S. Plastic Corporation to a foundation to fund God's work. If he agreed, God would own 100 percent of the company that Stanley had founded. In exchange, God was allowing Stanley to help millions of people hear about Jesus Christ.

Stanley could have chosen to retain his ownership and personally benefit from the company's profits, but he decided to seek God and his kingdom first. Many years later, I asked Stanley if he ever regretted that decision. He smiled as he said, "More than $200 million has been funneled into evangelistic efforts worldwide. God has allowed me to be a part of millions of people hearing the gospel. I made the right choice."

God may not ask you or me to give up all of our business, but he does desire for us to seek the kingdom of God first. If we do, we can count on him to do his part. He will take from you the worries of the world.

Stanley quickly learned about God's faithfulness. After he obediently signed over his stock to the foundation, God made it clear that the company needed a building four times larger than its existing facility. But God wanted it built without debt! Stanley started construction with $600,000 in the bank for a $3 million facility. Months later, the building was completed with no debt, and the company still had $600,000 in the bank.

I often recommend to entrepreneurs that they read Stanley's book *God Owns My Business*. If you seek God first, he will provide for everything you might need, but there are many other benefits to seeking God first. Let's look at four reasons.

Four reasons to seek God first

God owns it all. Psalm 24:1 teaches, "The earth is the Lord's, and all it contains, the world, and those who dwell in it." Stanley Tam learned that God's plan is so much better than ours. When we release our need to control the organization to the divine all-knowing power of God, the results will be far greater than we can imagine. Shouldn't we ask the owner his desire for his property?

Glorify God. If you ask most business leaders about their thoughts on the purpose of business, they will usually tell you that its only purpose is profit. However, in Colossians 3:17, the Apostle Paul wrote, "Whatever you do in word or deed, do all in the name of the Lord Jesus, giving thanks through him to God the Father." God has provided us the talents, abilities, and resources to carry out our vocational calling with excellence. Shouldn't we seek his will and then give him the glory for the outcome?

God is the fountain of knowledge. Many people will pay significant fees to hire consultants, yet they rarely turn to the fountain of all knowledge and wisdom. King Solomon wrote about God in Ecclesiastes 2:26: "For to a person who is good in His sight He has given wisdom and knowledge and joy, while to the sinner He has given the task of gathering and collecting so that he may give to one who is good in God's sight."

For many years, other organizations have referred business counseling calls to our ministry. When talking with the client, I've learned to pause and pray for God's divine wisdom. It still amazes me as to some of the thoughts and ideas that come from my mouth after seeking God's wisdom. He often provides just the right pearl of wisdom to help the caller through a tough situation.

God will judge every action. King Solomon spent the book of Ecclesiastes reflecting upon the meaning of his life. In the final chapter, the wisest man on earth wrote, "Fear God and keep His commandments, because this applies to every person. For God will bring every act to judgment, everything which is hidden, whether it is good or evil." You can choose to seek your interest first, but those choices will someday be judged by the Creator. Shouldn't you seek him and his kingdom first?

How to seek God first at work

When Nehemiah began his journey of rebuilding the walls of Jerusalem, he started by seeking God first. He prayed and fasted for four months before taking any other action. The result was a wall rebuilt in only fifty-two days, but also a spiritual revival that had been prophesied for thousands of years.

If you desire to build a business God's way, you need to begin by seeking God first *personally*. Following are four practical ways to seek God first.

- Establish and maintain proper priorities
- Pray
- Listen to God
- Understand and apply God's Word to your workplace

Establish and maintain proper priorities

Although life has seasons when it may be necessary to invest more time in a certain facet of your life than at other times—such as when you start a new business—overall we need to have the right priorities in place. If our priorities get skewed, we can end up chasing the wrong goals and objectives.

It was my third and final interview. I had been asked to consider becoming the chief lending officer for a bank that had a significant portfolio of bad loans. The bank president was being stripped of his CEO role and a new CEO had been appointed. During that final interview, I learned for the first time that if I accepted the position I would be working for this new CEO.

Naturally, I was curious about this new manager and his background, so I asked him to share about himself. "Rick," he said, "if you're going to work with me, you probably need to know my priorities. God's first, my family's second, and this bank is third."

At that time in my life, I was puzzled as to how he thought he could run a bank if it was so low on his priority list. Over time I began to understand how his priorities shaped his decisions and his life. Watching him model those priorities in his daily life made me desire to do likewise.

What does it mean to put God first? I have learned the hard way what it **doesn't** mean. It doesn't mean throwing yourself headlong into ministry or your vocational calling while sacrificing your family's needs. There was a season in my life when I thought putting God first meant doing whatever it took to keep my ministry going, regardless of what it cost my family. God allowed me to strain my marriage and wipe out our savings before he revealed to me that putting him first doesn't necessarily mean putting ministry or his work first.

Instead, putting God first is about the relationship I have with my Heavenly Father. The time I invest with God is my priority, not the work I try to do for him. In a moment we will discuss some ideas for enhancing your relationship with God, but let me discuss the other two priorities first.

As we discussed in the last chapter about taking care of employees, 1 Timothy 5:8 says, "But if anyone does not provide for his own, and especially for those of his household, he has denied the faith and is worse than an unbeliever." It is very important when we are doing work that we love to remember that our first and most important ministry is to our own family. We need to provide for them financially, spiritually, and emotionally. You can't do that if you are consumed with work.

God calls us to do our work with sincerity of heart as unto the Lord, but it's important that we don't let this priority creep into second or even first place in our priorities. Many business leaders work every day of the week and don't give their body the rest it needs. God designed us to take one day a week to rejuvenate our mind and body. So work hard five to six days a week, being engaged and passionate while you're there, but don't allow your passion to overtake your relationship with God and your family seven days a week.

Pray

My daughter, Megan, was interviewing for a position in a hospital when the HR director asked her a question that surprised her: "If you were in a meeting that opened with a prayer, would you be offended?" My daughter just smiled and said that she would be fine with prayer. The director responded, "That's good because we believe in the power of prayer here."

How much do you believe in the power of prayer? As a leader in an organization, we need to have God's power leading our life. The way we tap into that power is through our personal prayer life. In addition, we should be a model of prayer to others. Those we lead need to see that our decisions are founded in God's wisdom, which we receive through our time in prayer.

James 5:16 teaches, "The effective prayer of a righteous man can accomplish much." So how can we make our prayers effective?

Find your "secret place." Jesus said in Matthew 6:6: "But you, when you pray, go into your inner room, close your door and pray to your Father who is in secret, and your Father who sees *what is done* in secret will reward you." Find a place that is private and comfortable where you can consistently spend time with your Heavenly Father.

Delight yourself in the Lord. Psalm 37:4 teaches us: "Delight yourself in the Lord and He will give you the desires of your heart." When my daughter, Megan, was about three years old, she would wait at the door for me when I came home from work. She would sometimes squeal with glee as she reached for me to pick her up and spend time with her. It filled my heart with incredible joy and love for her. When we delight ourselves in God with that kind of childlike innocence, I believe our Father feels the same way.

Talk with God, not at him. One time I had a conversation with a man who talked about himself nonstop for ninety minutes. He never asked about me or why I was meeting with him. I felt used and frustrated. There have been many times when I'm sure I made God feel the same way. I talk about my issues nonstop with him, without ever realizing that this is a two-way relationship. God has a plan that is much better than any of my plans. Shouldn't I be willing to ask him about his agenda for our time together?

Line your will up with God's will. Our agendas can easily get in the way of God's agenda, but he knows all things and therefore, his plan is best. If we aren't willing to lay down our plans and selfish interests, then we will not likely be able to move forward in God's best plan. We need to seek God's forgiveness for any unconfessed sin that hinders us from hearing his will, and make peace with anyone who feels they have been wronged by us. We also need to lay down our agenda and ask God to reveal his agenda to us. It's then that we can petition God for the things we need and know that he will hear and respond. That is when our prayers really become effective.

Listen to God

Listening to God normally would be discussed in our conversation about prayer, but it's so important—yet so challenging for many—that we need to address it separately. Psalm 37:7 teaches, "Be still before the Lord and wait patiently for him." For many of us, it is a challenge to be quiet and wait. We are used to being busy and on the move with very little time to sit quietly and wait on God for his directives. Here are some ideas that may help.

Journaling. Many people have discovered that keeping a journal can be helpful in hearing from God and documenting thoughts. Sometimes I use journaling to take notes on what I believe I'm hearing from God in my quiet time. Other times I use journaling as a tool to record what I'm learning from God through studying his Word. It keeps my mind engaged on God while helping me document what God might be saying to me.

Fasting. Jesus said, "When you fast" not **if** you fast. Fasting is a tool that can be used to hear from God in a way that can release us from all sorts of bondage. Isaiah 58 teaches, "Is not this the kind of fasting I have chosen: to loose the chains of injustice and untie the cords of the yoke, to set the oppressed free and break every yoke?" Not only can fasting help us hear from God, but as a side benefit, scientists from the University of Southern California discovered that three-day fasts can regenerate the entire immune system. When we fast, we are more likely to be in tune with God and more prone to listen.

Understand and apply God's Word to the workplace

If we desire to order our priorities and seek God first in all we do—including in our workplace–it becomes critical that we understand God's Word and how it relates to what we do in the workplace. Here are a few thoughts that may help you to better understand God's principles relative to your vocation.

> *As you study Scripture in the future, begin considering each passage from the perspective of how it might be applied practically to your work life.*

Study God's Word through the eyes of a business person. When you've read God's Word in the past, you might have been thinking about a passage through the lens of a spouse or parent, or maybe as a leader in your church, but what if you studied it through the eyes of a business leader? For example, instead of applying Matthew 18:15–17 as just a way to resolve conflicts in the church, what if you realized the value of using it to resolve relational conflicts in your workplace? Suddenly God's Word becomes practical for your workplace. As you study Scripture in the future, begin considering each passage from the perspective of how it might be applied practically to your work life.

Understand the context. We have all heard people take a passage of God's Word out of context and twist it to their own interest. If we desire God's Word to be as beneficial as possible, it needs to be used within the context God intended. This means that when you study a passage, you need to determine

- o   who wrote it and who it was written to,
- o   the context in which it was written,
- o   when was it written,
- o   where they were located,
- o   why was it written, and
- o   how it is relevant to today.

In addition, it's critical that we look at Scripture as a whole. God is consistent in his themes throughout the Bible so if you read a passage that seems to contradict other passages, then it's likely you are misunderstanding the context.

Look for principles. As you study Scripture, it's helpful to realize that every word has a purpose. If you are reading a story about something that happened thousands of years ago, it could appear not to have much value to today's workplace. But if you look for the underlying principle in the story, it suddenly can be timeless guidance that's very appropriate to today. Ask yourself what you can learn from each passage to help you become trained on digging out valuable principles which are usable even today.

Apply principles wisely. There are commands in God's Word, but there are even more principles. Principles are guidelines that work well over the long haul, but which may not always prove out the way that you hope in the short term. This is because God has given us free will. Someone else may choose to ignore God's wisdom and cause you harm even if you applied his principles. That doesn't mean you don't use God's principles; it just means you need to be wise when applying them, and realize that when others are involved, you might have to rely on God's long-term plan to bring justice to your situation.

Summary

Hopefully these steps will help you order your priorities and assure that you are seeking God first. Unfortunately, even the most disciplined followers of Jesus can have difficulty in discerning God's will at times. During those times, pray, seek wise unbiased counsel, study God's Word, and keep your eyes wide open for the circumstances around you immediately after you pray. God may show you an answer and affirm it through the methods we have discussed. Develop the spiritual habits above and God will lead you on an exhilarating adventure.

CHAPTER FOUR

Leading with Integrity

"What does the Lord your God require of you, but to fear the Lord your God, to walk in all his ways, to love him, to serve the Lord your God with all your heart and with all your soul."
Deuteronomy 10:12

For about 140 years, God's beautiful city of Jerusalem had been lying in ruins due to the Israelites' disobedience of God's commands. The result? They were exiled to Babylon and their city was ransacked. Over time they seemed to have grown accustomed to their plight and were active as if God did not exist. That is, until Nehemiah showed up with an unlikely vision of restoring Jerusalem to its former beauty and stature!

Remarkably in only fifty-two days, the walls around Jerusalem were rebuilt, leaving little doubt that God **did** exist and had participated in this important work. It was so evident that even Israel's enemies realized it. In Nehemiah 6:16 we read, "When all our enemies heard of it, and all the nations surrounding us saw it, they lost their confidence; for they recognized that this work had been accomplished with the help of our God."

Israel's enemies realized God had shown up; now it was time for Israel to realize it and to begin changing their behavior. Nehemiah asked Ezra to drag out God's Word and share it with the people. For hours the people stood in reverence as they listened and became convicted by God's directives. Then something amazing happened. The entire audience fell on their knees and wept as they realized how far they had strayed from God and his commands.

In a matter of days, all of Israel publicly acknowledged that God existed, but they also acknowledged their sin against him and lined up to sign a covenant to begin obeying the commands they had been ignoring for decades. More importantly, they took action to change their behaviors and business practices to be in alignment with God's commands.

> *If you aren't modeling integrity then you can't expect your team to do any better than the example you set.*

Many people today wonder if our character is only shaped by our genetics. They also wonder if it's possible to train people to have integrity. I've shared the above story of Israel's transformation to remind us that if an entire nation can change their behavior and become people of integrity, then there certainly is hope for you and me and our modern day workplaces! But changed behavior can only come from changed beliefs.

If you desire to build a business God's way, it's critical that you lead with integrity. It all starts with you! If you aren't modeling integrity, then you can't expect your team to do any better than the example you set.

In this chapter, we are going to define integrity, discuss the different ways people make ethical decisions, and show you how you to implement a personal plan to assure you live a life that leads with integrity.

What is integrity?

According to *The American Heritage® Dictionary of the English Language, Fourth Edition*, integrity means "steadfast adherence to a strict moral or ethical code." This definition begs the question, "To whose moral code are we going to adhere?"

The word comes from the Latin root "integra," which means wholeness or completeness. The nature of the word demands an adherence to a set of values in all parts of our lives. For this to occur, it has to flow from the heart. Our motives are critical in determining whether we are walking with integrity holistically, or if we are putting on a good show for others. But it also requires that we are clear as to what code of ethics we are using as our guide.

Before we discuss what code we should follow, you might wonder why integrity is so important. Its importance in business is similar to the reasons we need laws in society. Without them, chaos and lawlessness prevail. Likewise in business, if we have no standards of conduct, then anything goes and trust is undermined. Since trust is the backbone of commerce, your business is at risk of folding without it.

How do most people make ethical decisions?

Shortly after September 11, 2001, the Barna Group conducted research to determine how people make ethical decisions. Although there were ten possible answers, the results can easily be grouped into four big categories:

- My personal code of ethics
- My family's code
- Other people's code
- God's code

My personal code. Roughly 46 percent of the people surveyed claimed that they make ethical decisions based on either what felt right to them personally or what brought them personal gain. Do you want your business' moral foundation built on everyone making decisions based on their own feelings? We read in the paper every week of businesses harmed and people going to prison for making ethical decisions based on their personal desires.

This criteria concerns me if this is what most of our workplace decisions are based upon. Even worse, this survey broke out the results for those eighteen to thirty-five years of age. Their answers for this category soared to 57 percent. This age group is now leading many of our organizations.

My family's code. Nearly 20 percent of the participants in this study claimed that their family impacted their ethical decisions. This might be good, but if you're trying to build a strong moral foundation in your business, do you want to rely on the family values of each person? One of my acquaintances spent nine years in prison because he made his business decisions based on his family's values. His family was part of the Mafia.

Other people's code. Approximately 16 percent of those surveyed wanted to make others happy, so they based their decisions accordingly. This happens many times in the workplace when your boss pressures you to do something immoral or your peers lean on you to conform. These decisions rarely have a good outcome and put an entire workplace at risk.

God's code. Only 13 percent of those surveyed claim they make their ethical decisions according to the Bible. Although we have all debated, at times, how best to interpret certain passages, we have to admit that this book has been used for moral decision making for thousands of years, and is the foundation for most of the laws created in America and many other societies. It's a standard that can be applied more consistently than any other, and when you consider the core of God's law is to love God and others, it's much more focused on doing what's best for the community as a whole.

Personally, I have had experience in my lifetime using each of these four methods. At eight years old, I was baptized mainly to please my mother. Over the next few years, I based my decisions on my family values, doing all that I could to please my mother. It usually kept me out of trouble.

When I was twelve, an extended family member introduced me to drinking, girls, deception, and dangerous activities. Suddenly my decisions migrated towards adhering to peer pressure and whatever pleased me personally. This led to poor decisions and harmed many people around me.

While in college, I was working for a construction company during the summers to pay for school. A co-worker revealed that he had been filling up his personal car at the gas station we used for the company truck and charging it to the company. The next summer when I returned from school and found myself at that same gas station, I succumbed once again to what pleased me personally. I filled up my car with gas and charged it to the company.

One day my boss asked me to come to the office. As I walked toward the office, I saw the owner of the business standing behind my car, writing down my license plate number. That was the longest walk of my life as I realized what was about to happen. As the embarrassment of getting fired washed over me, my ethical thinking changed slightly. Instead of striving to please *only* me, I decided I never wanted to experience that kind of humiliation again, so I would do whatever possible to please my bosses and assure I never lost another job.

This new ethic worked okay for several years until I began working at a CPA firm. While there a short time, one of the partners called me into his office. He informed me that the tax return I had worked on weeks before was wrong due to new information. He then informed me that rather than correct the return, he wanted me to doctor the work documents so that they tied to the incorrect tax return. What he was asking of me was illegal, but I was driven to please my boss so that I didn't lose my job. I did what he asked, but I suddenly realized that my ethical decision was putting me and the firm at risk of future trouble, not to mention violating government regulations.

By that time, I had tried most of the major ethical decision-making methods listed here, but they all left me feeling more *un*ethical than ethical. In 1990, that all changed. I had taken a job as chief lending officer for a bank who had brought in a new president. He had the most unique style of business I had ever experienced. When I needed answers, he often referred me to the Bible as a guide. What surprised me was how well these decisions kept playing out. But I was living a selfish life and had been running from God for decades.

Months later, while on vacation in Hawaii, God decided it was time to get my attention. While boogie boarding with my brother-in-law, I was suddenly sucked into a riptide that pulled me out to sea. After about an hour of doing everything I could to return to shore, I felt hopeless. All I could see were the very top of the high rises, which made me suspect that I was about a mile off shore. I unleashed myself from the boogie board's band, but a large wave took my board off into the distance. As I panicked and began swimming to retrieve it, my legs cramped.

Suddenly, I had nothing to hang onto. Any hope I had of surviving was evaporating. For the first time in many years, I turned to God. At that moment I realized that I was totally at his mercy. I feared that God could choose to take my life, leaving my wife and six-month-old daughter to fend for themselves. Out of my newfound reverence for God and his power, I asked him to give me another chance at life. Miraculously, he sent wave after wave to drive me close enough to shore for two young boys on a surfboard to reach me. They fished me out of the ocean, laid me across their surfboard, paddled me to shore, and dumped me on the beach.

When my wife found me, I told her that we were going to find a church and get right with God. That day I realized how real God was and that he had me in the palm of his hand. He could have ended my life, but instead, he chose to give me a second chance. Because of that experience, I have a different way of making ethical decisions today. I now understand what the Bible means when it urges us to both fear God and love him.

In Exodus 20:20 we read, "Moses said to the people, "Do not be afraid. God has come to test you, so that the fear of God will be with you to keep you from sinning." My experience with the power of God and how I was completely at his mercy helped me to understand this verse. It's the fear of God that will help keep me from sinning. It's the love of God and what he did for me that day, however, that gives me the motivation to want to please him.

Since that day, there have been occasions when a boss asked me to do something immoral. But rather than agree as I once did, I have learned that God sees all things and I need to fear and revere his power. Then out of my love for him, choose to honor him in all my choices.

The world's view vs. God's view

Moral relativism is the prevailing worldview. This mindset claims that whatever you think is right is right. If I think something else is right, then that's right, as well. How logical thinkers can actually buy into that philosophy is amazing to me. To assume that there are no moral absolutes leaves us at risk of chaos and a crumbling economic system. Trust is the backbone of commerce. When everyone begins doing business according to whatever pleases them personally, it undermines trust. Bribes and corruption become more commonplace, and as we see in many third world countries, it becomes more difficult to build a vibrant economic system.

God's view is different. God has established moral standards for us in his Word and has made it clear that the foundation of God's ethics ties back to what he told the Israelites in Deuteronomy 10:12: "What does the Lord your God require of you, but to fear the Lord your God, to walk in all his ways, to love him, to serve the Lord your God with all your heart and with all your soul."

If you asked me what differentiates God's view and the world's view on integrity, I would say it is the "fear of God." It's this one attribute that has helped me to make the right ethical decision when—in my past—I would have either chosen what pleased me personally or would have buckled to pressure from others.

Five workplace snares

A 2014 Ethics Resource Center study identified the top five ethical workplace issues. These included:

1. *Misusing company time.* People spend significant time during the workday on all sorts of activities that distract from the mission of the organization. Social media and the internet, in general, also are consuming vast amounts of work hours.

2. *Abusive behavior.* Rather than show employees the dignity and respect they deserve, there are still a large number of bosses who believe employees are for their use and abuse.

3. *Employee theft.* The fastest growing crime in America is employee theft. One out of forty employees steals from his or her employer.

4. *Lying to employees.* One out of five employees has been lied to in the last year. Remember, to many employees, a broken promise becomes a lie when they no longer believe an employer intends to honor that promise.

5. *Violating company internet policies.* More than 60 percent of employees visit websites each day that are unrelated to work.

The solution

True integrity is all about behavior. Thoughts and worldview must change before there will be any change in behavior. If you desire to build your business God's way, you first need to have God's worldview, and then apply it to all aspects of your business. This also will model for others what is expected of them. Here are four steps that can help you lead with integrity.

Study the Bible regularly. Back to the Bible ministry conducted a study on the effects on negative behavior when one regularly studies God's Word. They learned that four times a week or more of Bible study has a very significant impact on personal behaviors. Less than that had negligible impact.

For example, viewing pornography and extramarital affairs decreased 59 percent for those who were in the Word at least four times a week. Lying decreased 28 percent, and lashing out in anger decreased 31 percent. If you desire to decrease the poor ethical behavior in your workplace, model it first by studying God's Word daily, and find ways to encourage your team to do likewise.

Make an unwavering commitment to God. In Daniel 1:8 we read, "But Daniel resolved not to defile himself with the royal food and wine, and he asked the chief official for permission not to defile himself this way." It was Daniel's unwavering commitment to God that gave him the strength, courage, and God's favor for him to find solutions to his ethical dilemmas. When he committed not to defile himself with food sacrificed to other gods, he pursued alternatives, persistently requested help, and prayed and received God's favor. In your workplace, your values will be tested. If you do not make an unwavering commitment to conducting business God's way, you will likely stray.

Flee temptation. Joseph was tempted by a beautiful woman, but she was the wife of his boss. Rather than stay and run the risk of his fleshly desires winning out, he literally fled the building. Sometimes fleeing temptation is physically fleeing, other times it's looking for God's escape hatch. In 1 Corinthians 10:13, Paul teaches, "No temptation has overtaken you except what is common to mankind. And God is faithful; he will not let you be tempted beyond what you can bear. But when you are tempted, he will also provide a way out so that you can endure it."

Develop and rely on an accountability team. Daniel had Shadrach, Meshach, and Abednego. David had the prophet Nathan. We all are weak and likely to stumble without help. We need to surround ourselves with friends who not only care about our well-being, but who will also step into the uncomfortable role of asking us the tough questions. Spouses, close friends, and even peers at work can all become good accountability partners who help us to stay on track loving God and others.

Summary

Leading with integrity is the most critical step you can take to build an organization God's way. Understanding the power that comes from fearing and loving God will give you the ethical boost you need to gain the respect of your team. If you fear God, study his Word regularly, make an unwavering commitment to him, flee temptation, and develop accountability, you will become the leader that many look to as an example.

CHAPTER 5
Modeling Excellence

"Whatever you do, work at it with all your heart, as working for the Lord, and not for human masters, since you know that you will receive an inheritance from the Lord as a reward. It is the Lord Christ you are serving."
Colossians 3:23–24

As one of Larry's first customers, we experienced his excellent lawn maintenance service for years. His bright red trucks with white branding were always clean and well maintained. His service was thorough, and his team members always acted and dressed professionally. Larry and his team's level of quality always left us feeling confident we had made the right selection.

Even after proving himself in the industry and to the community, Larry came to the conclusion one evening that something was missing. He had attended an *Integrity Resource Center* dinner where he heard a speaker share about a nationally known company and how they had chosen to honor God—not only with excellent service—but also by giving him credit for their success. The next morning Larry called me and said, "Rick, that company is much larger than we are, yet they are bold about giving God the credit for their excellent products and services. Why can't we do that?"

This phone call led to Larry and I discussing how his company could better honor God. The end result was training for his staff and a new mission statement: "To serve God by helping our clients create beautiful, sustainable environments while we create opportunities for our associates and business partners." Larry wanted his entire team to know they were working first and foremost for the Lord. That is an example of how God defines excellence differently from the world.

What is excellence?

In business, excellence commands a premium. When we

God created each of us with a purpose in mind, skills uniquely designed to fulfill that purpose, and all of it with the intent that God would receive the glory from our demonstration of excellence.

see high quality products and services, we usually expect to pay more than competing brands. The nature of excellence is to receive products or services that exceed what is typically expected, which means increased value for the customer.

However, some people equate excellence with perfection. Excellence is above-average service that may aim for perfection, but perfection will not be attained. We live in a fallen world. Although God desires for us to strive for perfection, he does not expect us to reach it. Excellence is a journey, but perfection is the destination.

For most people in business, the motive behind excellence is to either enhance their bottom line or to have a moment of glory for the individual performing the service. However, God's view on excellence is different. God created each of us with a purpose in mind, skills uniquely designed to fulfill that purpose, and all of it with the intent that God would receive the glory from our demonstration of excellence. Colossians 3:17 summarizes this concept when it states, "Whatever you do, whether in word or deed, do it all in the name of the Lord Jesus, giving thanks to God the Father through him."

When God believes he is going to properly receive the glory and credit, he can join in the work in such a unique way that the results far exceed our wildest expectations. When

Nehemiah set out to rebuild the walls around Jerusalem, he made it clear to God that it was Nehemiah's desire to please God by helping rebuild the city. Nehemiah wasn't in it for his own glory; he desired that would be God pleased and receive the glory. It's because of that motive, God did something so remarkable that the world is still amazed by the result.

In Nehemiah 6 we read, "So the wall was completed on the twenty-fifth of Elul, in fifty-two days. When all our enemies heard about this, all the surrounding nations were afraid and lost their self-confidence because they realized that this work had been done with the help of our God." When we do our part and work with all of our heart as unto the Lord, that leaves the door wide open for God to do *his* part in such a profound way that the world marvels at the result.

The ingredients of excellence

As a leader in your organization, you set the tone for the entire organization. This includes modeling excellence. If you desire to excel in your business, there are a variety of ingredients that need to be stirred together to create excellent products and services. By embracing and modeling these ingredients, you set the pace for the remainder of your team to strive towards excellence, as well. The ingredients for biblical excellence include:

- Purpose
- Skill
- Attitude
- Christ-centered labor
- Serving well

Purpose

The Apostle Paul taught us in Ephesians 2:10, "For we are God's handiwork, created in Christ Jesus to do good works, which God prepared in advance for us to do." It's hard for some to imagine, but God created each of us with a purpose in mind. Many have the flawed view that only pastors and missionaries are called by God. It's clear from this verse and many others in the Scriptures that this is not true.

God ordained a plan for each of us and he has work, including our regular vocation, scheduled in advance for us to complete. Sometimes that purpose may not be as glamorous as we might like, or we may have an assignment that is mostly preparation for our future, but even that points us towards our purpose.

Nehemiah was a cupbearer to the king. Although this was a very important role, especially since the king he was serving virtually ruled the world at the time, God was using Nehemiah in that role to prepare him for the important work of restoring Jerusalem physically and spiritually. For Jerusalem to be restored, it would require the king's favor, significant resources, and enough authority to persuade the people to help. God pre-ordained Nehemiah to work for the king so that when the time was right, Nehemiah would have the favor to accomplish his next assignment.

God has a plan and a purpose for your vocation. If you do not yet know what that purpose is, I encourage you to pray, examine your past work experiences and trends, seek counsel from people who know you well, and look at your current employment situation relative to your strengths and passions.

Skill

In Exodus 31:6, God explained about the skills of his people when he said, "In the hearts of all who are skillful I have put skill, that they may make all that I have commanded you." In the same chapter, we learn that God gave a man named Bezalel the spirit of God with skills, abilities, and knowledge to do all sorts of crafts, including building the Ark of the Covenant. I don't believe that Bezalel was unique in that regard. God also has created you with unique skills.

If you question what they are you can ask your spouse, close friends, or peers what they believe to be your best skills. They will likely know things about you that you may undervalue. One other way is to be aware of the types of requests for help you receive from others. If different people seek you out for a certain kind of help, it's because they perceive you as being strong in that area. That is a God-given skill you should use as frequently as possible. When you do, Proverbs 22:29 teaches, "Do you see a man skilled in his work? He will stand before kings; he will not stand before obscure men."

Attitude

One of the most common, yet most overlooked factors in excellence is attitude. Many people carry around "head trash" from past experiences that hinders them from living up to their full potential. Just when things are going well, many people unknowingly and quietly sabotage themselves because they do not feel worthy of the success they are experiencing.

Philippians 4:8 says, "Finally, brethren, whatever is true, whatever is honorable, whatever is right, whatever is pure, whatever is lovely, whatever is of good repute, if there is any excellence and if anything worthy of praise, dwell on these things." God desires us to have a positive attitude. If we desire to model excellence, others will make note of our attitude. If our attitude is positive and affirming, it will encourage others and lead them towards being positive, as well.

Christ-centered Labor

A pastor in Portland, Oregon, decided to start a church in the urban core. He decided funding in that part of town would be difficult, so he took a unique approach. He started a hotel. The hotel became the facility for their church meetings, as well as an important way to fund the ministry. The hotel was wildly successful, leading the church to plant churches and hotels in other cities, as well.

According to this pastor, the key to their hotel's success was Christ-centered labor. Every employee was trained in customer service with a very focused approach: "If Jesus walked through our hotel doors today," the pastor would tell his team, "how fast and how well would you serve him? Remember that for every customer because we are serving the Lord with every customer that walks through the door."

This hotel has become renowned for its customer service because management realized the difference between the world's idea of customer service and God's idea. Colossians 3 has a great customer service mantra: "Whatever you do, work at it with all your heart, as working for the Lord, not for human masters, since you know that you will receive an inheritance from the Lord as a reward. It is the Lord Christ you are serving."

Serving Well

In 1 Timothy 3:13, the apostle Paul said to church elders, "Those who have served well gain an excellent standing and great assurance in their faith in Christ Jesus." I believe this is just as appropriate for leaders of organizations as it is for elders of the church. Excellence demands that we serve well. Whether you are the leader of an organization or an employee, excellence still requires serving well with sincerity of heart.

Colossians 3 teaches, "Slaves, obey your earthly masters in everything; and do it, not only when their eye is on you and to curry their favor, but with sincerity of heart and reverence for the Lord." God is willing to do his part if we do ours. We can—and should—pray and ask for God's help, but God typically accomplishes his goals by his people faithfully serving well in each task he has called them to complete.

Summary

Many people desire to be known for their excellence, yet few seem to rise to the challenge. God desires you to model excellence in and through the organization he has called you to lead. Before you move on to the next chapter, ponder these five questions:

1. What is my purpose vocationally?
2. What are my God-given skills?
3. Who am I working for and who gets the credit typically?
4. How would I describe my attitude?
5. How faithful am I at "serving well"?

Third Key:

Cultivating and Maturing Your Team

CHAPTER SIX
Developing Servant Leaders

"If anyone wants to be first, he must be the very last,
and the servant of all."
Mark 9:35

My whole philosophy on leadership changed the day my boss—the bank president—washed my car. There wasn't a special event or any particular reason. He just told the employees to bring their cars around and he would spend the day washing them.

It seemed foolish to me—we should probably be washing *his* car rather than him washing ours–but that act, coupled with his overall servant attitude on a regular basis, built a loyalty that paid great dividends. He later went on to be president of a new bank, and a large number of staff asked if they could follow him due to their loyalty. He was one of the first leaders I'd met with a real servant's heart.

> Two of the most important qualities in a servant leader are humility and obedience to God.

Two of the most important qualities in a servant leader are humility and obedience to God. Judges 6-8 tells about a humble and obedient leader who had remarkable results. We're told that the Israelites once again had done evil in the eyes of God, so for seven years he turned them over to the Midianites. The story says that the Midianites were so oppressive that the Israelites had to hide out in caves and shelters in the mountains. Not only did they suffer through poor living conditions, but they were aggravated, tormented, and beginning to starve.

Read what scripture tells us in Judges 6:3–6: "Whenever the Israelites planted their crops, the Midianites, Amalekites and other eastern peoples invaded the country. They camped on the land and ruined the crops all the way to Gaza and did not spare a living thing for Israel, neither sheep nor cattle nor donkeys. They came up with their livestock and their tents like swarms of locusts. It was impossible to count the men and their camels; they invaded the land to ravage it. Midian so impoverished the Israelites that they cried out to the Lord for help."

A military strategist would tell you they were in a pretty bleak situation. The Israelites were outnumbered, had poor food supply, very little resources, and a ruthless opponent. If there ever was a time to look around and find the meanest, strongest, and most fearless leader you could find, now was it. But God's ways are not our ways. He picked Gideon.

Gideon responded, "But Lord, how can *I* save Israel? My clan is the weakest in Manasseh, and *I* am the least in my family." Throughout most of the story we read of Gideon's fearfulness. Does this sound like the kind of leader you or I would choose to head up mission impossible? I think I would have been looking for someone else.

However, this story is full of examples of Gideon's servant attitude. Most leaders are constantly striving to grow their power base. Gideon had 32,000 men that wanted to follow him, but he downsized (with God's guidance) to 300. He could have sent out scouts, but he went himself. He could have sent men into battle before him, but **he** led the charge. He could have forced his men to execute prisoners, but he did it himself. He could have become king after the victory (the people asked him), but he declined.

What was the result of this humble—and sometimes fearful—leader's mission? Due to Gideon's obedience, 300 men conquered the Midianites, the Amalekites, and all the other eastern people who had settled in the valley as thick as locusts. Their camels could no more be counted than the sand on the seashore. This was done with a brilliant strategy that only the Lord could have orchestrated.

Why should we become a servant leader?

After reflecting on Gideon's situation, it is obvious the Israelites could have ignored Gideon and continued to be impoverished, or they could have picked the strongest, boldest leader among them and tried to defeat their enemy. Either way, the result would have been disastrous because it wasn't God's plan. If we become as humble and pure as children, then we can be used by God in a powerful way. By becoming God's *servant* we can become a leader that God can use in a profound way.

There is something about humility that allows us to listen to God. When we are leading by our own strength, we are not able to fulfill God's plan because we aren't likely to *discern* His plan. If we remember that we are children of God—his servants—then when he gives us directions, we will be more likely to listen and follow. Sometimes it won't make sense to us, but that's when we step out in faith and do it anyway.

Have you ever had a boss give you a task without any explanation about how it fits into the company's big picture? It's difficult to do it in a way you don't understand, and if you're like me, you may make all kinds of excuses and reasons why it's not important. Let me give you an example.

When I started a car rental agency years ago, I went to a bank to get a small business loan. I knew what amount and terms I thought I needed, and how I wanted it done. The bank's wise chief lending officer suspected I was undercapitalized and that things wouldn't go as I planned, so he made the loan proceeds only available to purchase cars. The bank would only finance 75 percent of the actual cost of the cars, and none of the loan proceeds could be used for working capital, which is the nice term for operating losses.

Later, I learned what great wisdom this was, not only for the bank, but also for me. That provision made it necessary for me to periodically stop and review the progress of the business. Eventually, I liquidated the business and paid off the bank and my other creditors. Had that stopgap not been in the loan requirements, I know I would have proceeded for another three to six months, right into bankruptcy. I later worked for that wise man at the bank, and had great respect his abilities.

God is like that wise old lender; he knows where we are headed and why we need to do the things he's asking us to do, even when it doesn't make sense. He also knows that he can't always disclose to us why. Sometimes it's because we are stubborn and won't understand until we've learned the hard way. Other times it's because we are not strong enough to be told what the future holds.

So why should we be a servant leader? Here are three good reasons:

1. The humility of a servant leader makes us more teachable.
2. The obedience of a servant leader gets us God-sized results.
3. Servant leadership builds and strengthens relationships, resulting in more people willing to follow and serve your mission.

Who should we serve?

Most people say they are in business to serve the customer. Is the customer the only one we are to serve? I think not. Jesus taught that we are to serve our neighbor, and his definition of neighbor was a whole lot broader than what I often care to remember. It includes everyone around us. In business that means our customers, suppliers, employees, bosses, board of directors, prospects, creditors, and anyone else that we stumble across. That is a hard thing to implement when your customer is complaining, an employee just cost you a large job, or a supplier just cut you off.

Employees

Nehemiah had been appointed as governor over Jerusalem by the king. It was typical for the people to be heavily taxed so that the governor could have extravagant feasts daily, and be treated like royalty. But Nehemiah was a servant leader. In Chapter 5 we read, "But the earlier governors—those preceding me—placed a heavy burden on the people and took forty shekels of silver from them in addition to food and wine. Their assistants also lorded it over the people. But out of reverence for God I did not act like that." Nehemiah cared for his people rather than take advantage of them for personal gain as those before him had.

As employers, our first obligation is to our employees. In many ways, the relationship between an employer and employee is similar to that of a father and child. God has entrusted that person to us, and we are called to be good stewards of the human resources, as well as the financial resources. If you believe that your business is similar to a family in terms of responsibilities, then 1 Timothy 5:8 can be very convicting: "If anyone does not provide for his immediate family, he has denied the faith and is worse than an unbeliever."

Nothing could be more humbling than gathering our employees and serving them to the point of taking off their shoes and washing their feet as Jesus did to the disciples. In today's culture, that would be similar to giving your lowest paid employee the keys to the company car, the country club membership, and the biggest office.

Customers

From a practical standpoint, customers need to be served and served well if we desire our business to prosper. In the last few years, we have given a great deal of lip service in this country to customer service and total quality management, but have been very poor on implementation. As smaller businesses have been gobbled up by the large ones, customer service has suffered. Sure, the big corporations give it lip service because they know Wall Street likes to hear the latest buzz words, but few actually care.

It is hard enough for a small business to stay close enough to their customers to show that they truly care, let alone a large corporation that is far removed from the front-line customer service representatives. Once when I chaired a quality service task force for a Fortune 500 company, I quickly learned that management wanted results they could point to and display for shareholders, but only if they didn't have to invest any time or energy into it.

The most commonly cited reason for failed quality service is lack of buy-in from senior management. People only do what they actually see is important to their superiors. If middle management knows that senior management isn't serious, what message do you think that conveys to staff?

A true servant attitude towards customers will only come from heart-felt concern by front-line employees. Heart-felt concern only comes from a system that truly recognizes, rewards, and encourages that sort of attitude. Businesses that take this seriously sell their customer service vision to their employees from the very first day. Then they sell it again the second day and every day thereafter by rewarding and encouraging the employees who demonstrate it to the customers, and by eliminating employees who don't.

Board

Few small businesses utilize a board of directors the way they are legally designed to operate. If your business is incorporated, you should have a board of directors to whom you are accountable and whom you serve. The board has the oversight function in a business. They are supposed to set the vision and keep management focused on the big picture purposes of the business. If you do not use these positions the way they were designed, it is likely there is no management accountability and the vision of the business becomes clouded.

In most states, legally the board can be simply the owner of the business. Especially in most small, closely-held corporations, that person can hold the title of president and secretary without any other officers. There are never real "board meetings" in these situations, but since you're legally required to have at least an annual meeting, the lawyers typically draft minutes of a meeting that never existed. After all, who wants to attend a meeting if you're the only person coming? But I think this mode of operation is one of the biggest mistakes a small business owner can make. There is definitely wisdom in many counselors, and to make a farce of the laws in this area—which were specifically designed for a wise reason—is a shame. I cannot tell you about all of the invaluable insight I have received from serving on boards.

Suppliers and creditors

According to the Bible, the borrower is servant to the lender. This is one of the few areas where business owners truly serve, and I can tell you from a lender's perspective, it is rarely ever cheerfully. Usually their service takes place out of requirements the lender places on them, either to get the loan, or to keep it from being called. One of the first practical rules I learned as a lender was never to give loan proceeds to a borrower before they provided all of the information and signed all of the documents. It was amazing how after the money was disbursed, it became almost impossible to get documents signed or additional information provided.

The Lord calls us to serve cheerfully as if we are serving him. This means that we need to be cooperative to suppliers and creditors, supplying them with whatever they might need, and especially providing open communication about our circumstances.

One of the biggest issues of conflict in vendor and creditor relationships is lack of communication. It is the norm, rather than the exception, that if a business cannot provide required disclosures or meet timelines to pay, then they will likely just ignore the situation and hope it goes away, rather than call the vendor to explain their circumstances.

Many people can find it in themselves to serve customers cheerfully, but the real witness comes from people who can serve their creditors cheerfully.

How to develop servant leaders

When a business grows quickly, it's easy to overlook servant leadership as one of the desired hiring traits in new leaders. It will require forethought and training of your team for the entire culture of the business to be known for its servant leadership. Here are five key considerations for training.

Change the paradigm. In Mark 9, Jesus taught his disciples in that they were to be a "servant to all." Many leaders believe they only need to serve their customer or their boss, but this limits their responsibility. They should also consider serving those who may report to them on the organizational chart.

Focus your team on the vision, mission, and values of your organization. When people become adept at being a servant to all, it's easy to have so many opportunities to serve that they lose sight of the mission. Constantly refreshing the message of your vision, mission, and values to team members will help them make wise decisions on how to invest their time and service to others.

Train them to look, ask, and listen. There are many service opportunities each day that we walk past without considering the possibilities. If you desire to have a servant's heart, you have to be willing to see and understand what may be right before you. This requires keeping your eyes open for those opportunities. You will also need to *ask* those around you how you might best serve them. Finally, you need to be a good listener to understand what they truly need and how you might best serve them.

Practice the Golden Rule. Doing unto others as you would have them do to you is a great motto for a servant leader. A team that keeps this key principle in the forefront of their thinking will know they have the freedom and permission to humbly serve others.

Reward and recognize servant hearts. The best way to build a team of servants is to publicly recognize and reward those who are modeling your desired values. On a regular basis, highlight those individuals who are performing remarkable service to others. It will continue to motivate them and those who witness the accolades.

Summary

Servant leadership is key to building a business God's way. Jesus modeled this amazing principle when he recruited a small team of leaders who multiplied his ministry to billions of people. Having a humble heart, an obedient spirit, and a desire to train others to do likewise will result in a healthy organization that honors God and serves all of your constituents profitably.

CHAPTER SEVEN
Cherishing Your Greatest Asset

"Masters, provide your slaves with what is right and fair,
because you know that you also have a Master in heaven."
Colossians 4:1

The greatest resource God gives us as leaders are the people under our care. In many businesses, this is the most overlooked and underused resource. Many tend to value financial results much more than the people whose lives their decisions affect.

Within the context of being a good steward of your business, it is important to recognize your responsibility as a shepherd over the flock God has entrusted to you. Is the golden rule being maintained in your relationship with your employees? Are you truly doing to them as you would want them doing unto you?

One of the reasons I believe Nehemiah was so effective was that he cared enough about his people that he constantly understood the pulse of the people. If they needed to be inspired with vision, he gave them vision. If they were trembling in fear, he reminded them that God was on their side. Even when they were overwhelmed with poverty, Nehemiah became their advocate. He cherished each person. Sometimes that meant he had to hold them accountable, other times he had to serve them.

People who work for you can make or break your business faster than anything else. Since many of the problems in managing people originate from poor communication, let's look at the seven phases of the employee process, from interviewing to firing.

Seven phases of employment

The typical seven of employee tenure are:

1. Interviewing
2. Hiring
3. Compensation
4. Training
5. Motivating employees\
6. Disciplining employees
7. Dismissing employees

Phase 1: Interviewing

When you realize you need to hire someone, don't make the mistake of charging into it so fast that you end up with a bigger problem than you were trying to solve. Begin by asking yourself some important questions.

1. What is the going rate of pay for this type of position? What can you afford to pay?
2. How will pay relate to the bottom-line productivity you hope to achieve?
3. Can you make the pay structure variable in nature?
4. Would an incentive pay structure be more effective?
5. Do you really need to hire someone or is there another way to accomplish the goal?
6. Could you outsource this job instead of adding what usually becomes permanent staff?
7. Are you certain that your current need is not a seasonal versus a permanent need?
8. Does it need to be part time or full time?
9. What skills are needed to fit the job?
10. What personality traits do you need to fit your team and type of job?

Be a good steward of your time and respect the time of those you interview by thinking through these questions in advance and developing a plan.

Five steps to effective interviewing

The goal of the interview process is to narrow the field of applicants to your best possible candidates. This requires a vision of the kind of person the next hire could be.

In Exodus 18, Moses was burned out from judging all of the cases for more than 600,000 Israelites. His father-in-law, Jethro, gave him some great advice in Exodus 18:21: "But select capable men from all the people–men who fear God, trustworthy men who hate dishonest gain–and appoint them as officials over thousands, hundreds, fifties, and tens."

Give thought to the kind of person you desire to hire using these five steps:

Pray. Ask God to bring to you the right applicants and to direct you with great discernment to make a good decision.

Develop the job description. It's critical that you put on paper exactly what your expectations are for the position you are trying to fill. Too many people begin interviewing without clarity on what actual responsibilities will be assigned to the new person. This can lead to frustration for both parties when the list of duties changes later and the new hire feels he/she has been duped.

Determine necessary talents and skills. Ideally you need to find a new hire that has God-given talents to complete the tasks you have assigned to him/her. This requires you to be clear on what talents and skills might be needed.

Develop interview questions. The best indicator of future performance usually comes from history. You should carefully develop questions that will reveal how the applicant has handled situations in the past so you have a sense of how they might handle them when they are working for you.

Use profiling tools. Personality profiles, strength assessments, and other resources help you quickly determine how the applicant typically tackles projects or interacts with others. However, don't forget that they are only tools, and should be used in conjunction with the other parts of the hiring process. Every person has been uniquely designed by God so no one fits perfectly into a profile. Total dependence upon profiling tools can cull out someone who might have been a great fit if all the factors are not carefully considered.

Phase 2: Hiring

Once you have determined what duties need to be performed, what kind of person you need to perform those duties, and have interviewed candidates, it is time to select and hire the right person. This requires some diligence.

In the book of Joshua, the Israelites learned the lesson of being diligent in their decisions by both seeking God's counsel and doing the necessary legwork to make the right decision. You can ask all the right questions and do the necessary due diligence, yet still be deceived if you do not seek the Lord's counsel. On the other hand, if you presume that your peaceful feelings are from the Lord, and don't do the proper due diligence, you are likely to find that you misread God's leading.

The four Cs of hiring

When I'm interviewing multiple candidates for a job, it can become too easy to get caught up in certain aspects of an individual or the chemistry you have with an applicant, and lose sight of the big picture. For that reason, I have developed four words to guide my process and thinking.

- Character

- Calling
- Competence
- Chemistry

Character

Character matters! You can hire the most competent financial person ever, but if their past character indicates they might be a crook, you will usually regret hiring them. Although some character assessment tools can be helpful, you will generally need to get some personal and professional references—then actually check them out.

One day a frustrated business owner called me for counsel. She told me that they had recently fired their bookkeeper for embezzling $40,000. The business owner went on to tell me that they had asked for—and received—references, but had never checked them out.

She called the references after they discovered the fraud. Every past employer she called had terminated this bookkeeper for theft. She said to me, "If only I had checked out the references before hiring the bookkeeper, I could have saved myself a lot of money and grief."

Prayer is also helpful in discovering someone's character. In 1 Samuel 16:7, we read about how Samuel almost selected the wrong king, instead of selecting David as king. "The Lord said to Samuel, 'Do not consider his appearance or his height, for I have rejected him. The Lord does not look at the things people look at. People look at the outward appearance, but the Lord looks at the heart.'" If you sincerely ask, God can reveal what you need to know about an applicant's character.

Calling

Ephesians 2:10 says, "For we are God's handiwork, created in Christ Jesus to do good works, which God prepared in advance for us to do." If God prepared work for us to do in advance, then each of us should have a purpose or calling from God. Someone simply looking for a paycheck will not likely perform at their optimum because they're not performing with passion.

It's important to note that many people do not know or understand that God has a calling for them vocationally. You may have to draw it out of them by asking about their passions, their interests, and what sort of work they have done in the past that has been easy and fun for them.

Competence

Although competence is sometimes overrated during the hiring process, it is still important to hire people who will be able to skillfully handle the job. If someone has the character and the calling, they can often be trained in competence, but finding someone with character, calling, *and* competence is a true treasure.

Examining past work history is important when trying to discern competence, but look deep enough to discover those traits and skills that may be transferable to the position you have available. Over the years, I have helped several pastors transition from working in a church to joining the marketplace. On a resume, their work experience may not look like a fit, yet when you look at the leadership skills, training expertise, and other duties they performed in that role, there are many positions in which they could work well.

Chemistry

Being aware of the organization's culture is critical for a team to work well together. To some extent, each new person added to a team changes that culture. If you find two candidates that both have strong character, seem called to that type of position, and are competent, then selecting the person who will have the best chemistry with the team only makes sense. When people can work in harmony and enjoy working together, it usually makes the workplace fun and more productive.

That being said, be sure to hire people with different personalities and styles to provide the diversity necessary for a healthy team. The Apostle Paul talked at length in Romans and in his letters to the Corinthians about how there are different body parts with different functions. The key is that the different parts need to work in unity and harmony, so when possible, look to hire those who will fit nicely with your culture.

A question I get asked by many business owners is whether they should only hire Christians. I think this is an issue that should be thought about and prayed for very carefully. There are occasions when you definitely should only hire believers, such as a church, para-church, or other forms of ministry. However, if businesses only hired Christians, they would primarily be ministering to each other with effectively no evangelism in the workplace. I know several business owners who derive great joy from the evangelism they are able to do right in their own workplace.

It is important to prayerfully consider what God desires to do through your business. If he wants to use it to witness to staff, then there's your answer. On the other hand, if you feel you are called to "feed his sheep," then you might be better served nurturing young believers in the faith. Whichever you feel called to do, remember that God desires excellence in the workplace.

Phase 3: Compensation

Once you have determined whom you would like to hire, compensation is usually the next big hurdle. When hiring someone, it is common to find out how much that person made in their last job, give them a small raise, and hire them. This approach is full of pitfalls. Let me give you an example.

Suppose you hire a bookkeeper for $20 an hour. Six months later it is time to hire another person with similar skills. The job market is tighter, so you hire the second bookkeeper for $25 an hour. She has similar skills as the first, but less experience.

After a couple of years, you promote the first bookkeeper to department head and give her a 15 percent raise. Of course, it's only a matter of time before she discovers that she's only making $23 an hour, but the second bookkeper, who now works for her, is making $25 an hour and neither are happy about the situation. "How did I get into this mess?" you ask yourself.

Taking another look at compensation

We have developed a pay system in corporate America that needs to be revisited. In order for businesses to remain competitive while still adhering to the golden rule, we need to develop a system that rewards people for their skill level and their part in the business's productivity and profitability.

Bonuses and cost of living raises that are not tied to performance or enhanced skills do almost nothing for motivation and developing an employee's potential, not to mention profits for the business. Cost of living raises actually perpetuate the need for further cost of living raises.

What if pay was made as variable as possible, but tied to the overall performance of the business, with raises given only for improved skills that add to the productivity of the business? Pay for performance will greatly reward your employees *and* your business as your staff finds they are able to give themselves a raise simply by working harder and more effectively. If they focus on goals that will actually *improve* the business's profitability and productivity, then the business will prosper, and they will share in the gain.

This requires a degree of disclosure on the business owner's part, which may be uncomfortable for some. Open book management is a topic often discussed in the Bible. During biblical times, most businesses were farm related. If you were a hired hand, you could see the harvest. It was pretty easy to determine how much grain was harvested and what it was worth.

In 1 Corinthians 9:7–10, Paul said: "Who serves as a soldier at his own expense? Who plants a vineyard and does not eat of its grapes? Who tends a flock and does not drink of the milk? Do I say this merely from a human point of view? Doesn't the Law say the same thing? For it is written in the Law of Moses: 'Do not muzzle an ox while it is treading out the grain.' Is it about oxen that God is concerned? Surely he says this for us, doesn't he? Yes, this was written for us, because when the plowman plows and the thresher threshes, they ought to do so in the hope of sharing in the harvest."

A biblical discussion on compensation cannot overlook minimum pay requirements. Deuteronomy 24:14 tells us, "You shall not oppress a hired servant who is poor and needy, whether he is one of your countrymen or one of your aliens who is in your land in your towns." Many businesses profit on the backs of their employees by paying the absolute minimum they can.

If we are good shepherds over the staff the Lord has blessed us to manage, then we should care for their well-being. A living wage should be paid to everyone. If you cannot afford to pay a living wage, then maybe you have the wrong person or a position that is not viable for the long term.

Phase 4: Training

Many businesses, especially smaller companies, overlook the importance of training. Too many times we hire a new employee expecting them to hit the ground running. We hand them a project without much direction and check back later, only to be disappointed that either the project is not done or it's done very poorly. Success doesn't just happen. Your people need training. The three primary types of training are

- New employee training
- Product and service training
- Personal development training

New employee training. A new hire's first training should be on the company culture, values, and policies. If you want this new hire to be an ambassador for your company, then it is imperative they fully understand what your company is about.

Product and service training. Your team needs to know about your company's products and services, their part in producing those, and how you make money on them.

Personal Development training. You also want your employees—who are so important to the future success of your business—to be as equipped as possible to develop into future leaders.

Since training dollars do not usually show immediate bottom-line results, it is often times difficult for entrepreneurs to turn loose of money for this purpose. However, study upon study has shown that companies that pay for additional training get more than their investment returned in increased productivity. Proverbs 13:13-14 teaches, "Whoever scorns instruction will pay for it, but whoever respects a command is rewarded. The teaching of the wise is a fountain of life, turning a person from the snares of death."

Examine the company's current and future needs so you can work out a plan to assist each employee with reaching their full potential. Identify—or have them identify—specific training possibilities for them to achieve those goals, and then budget time and money accordingly.

Phase 5: Motivating employees

Your team will flounder without motivated employees. Performance discussions are essential for open communication between employees and employers. Formalizing a process for performance reviews can be time well spent and help your team members better understand and drive towards your definition of success for their role.

When I became the new chief lending officer for a regional bank, I discovered there was very little structure and few HR policies. The employees who reported to me had all been told—once a year by the president—they were doing a good job, and then were given their annual raise.

Just like developing a plan for your business, employee performance reviews are a tool to help develop a plan for each employee. During the review, you should assess past performance, identify strengths and weaknesses, and map out a plan for the employee's future at the company. I have always appreciated bosses who cared enough about me to help me succeed even if that meant my next step was out of that job or even that company. The biblical approach to managing people is to desire success for your staff in spite of your self-interests.

The book of Exodus shows how Moses was hired by God to do a job. As I studied the book, I saw how God motivated Moses using these seven steps:

1. Set clear expectations
2. Provide necessary resources
3. Utilize their skills and talents
4. Have constant and open communication
5. Be sincerely concerned for the person
6. Encourage personal development

7. Reward behavior

Set clear expectations. God made it clear that Moses was to go to Egypt and set the Israelites free from bondage to the Egyptians. Likewise, your employees need to clearly know what you expect of them.

Provide necessary resources. When Moses wondered how he could possibly convince Pharaoh to let the Israelites go, God gave him a staff that performed miracles, and he provided his brother Aaron to help him speak to Pharaoh. At times, your team members will need resources to meet your expectations. Be prepared to provide what is necessary.

Utilize their skills and talents. Although Moses didn't realize it, his background in Pharaoh's home and as a humble shepherd were just the skills God used to accomplish the task. Know your people well enough to understand their skills and talents, then encourage them in those, leveraging them to reach your organizational goals.

Constant and open communication. God constantly answered Moses' questions and left the door open for Moses to ask for help when he needed it. Likewise, your people need to know that you are available to listen to their concerns and to provide direction.

Be sincerely concerned for the person. Throughout his journey, Moses was criticized and attacked by his own people. God went to bat for Moses, even striking Moses' sister with leprosy when she stirred up people against him. Your people need to know you are for them and that you have their back.

Encourage personal development. God knew Moses needed tremendous humility to carry out the task he had in mind. Moses spent forty years in the desert as a shepherd after he spent his earlier life living in Pharaoh's home. This helped him develop into an amazingly humble, yet powerful, servant leader.

You need to help identify the potential in your team members and encourage them to develop their strengths.

Reward behavior. Moses was faithful to carry out God's requests in spite of overwhelming odds. In return, God rewarded Moses with success in releasing the Israelites in ways that only God could provide. When your employees behave in the manner you have requested, you need to be prepared to generously reward their behavior.

One year I significantly outperformed my peers. When it came time for my raise, I was told I had done such a good job I was going to receive a raise at the top of the range allowed that year—a whopping 5 percent—instead of the 3 percent I would have received for nominal performance.

All my hard work and a significant bottom-line improvement for the company only gained me an additional 2 percent. You can imagine that I was not nearly as motivated the next year.

If we structure pay and rewards relative to performance, you will have some employees who will not receive any increase, which will also allow you more flexibility for the top performers. A cost of living increase is not paying for performance. Pay should somehow relate to the contribution of employees to the business. And don't forget recognition as one of the ways employees most want to be appreciated for their accomplishments.

Phase 6: Disciplining employees

Resolving conflict and disciplining employees is a difficult issue for many managers. Either they are afraid to resolve an issue, or they react abruptly to a situation without thought. Both of these approaches are damaging to the employer-employee relationship. If you need to resolve a conflict or discipline an employee, remember the Golden Rule and treat them as you would want to be treated. Here are some other points to remember:

Five suggestions for disciplining an employee
1. Do it promptly. Don't be rash, but don't let the conflict linger.
2. Use Matthew 18 as a model. Jesus told his disciples to go one on one, then two on one, then finally take them to those in authority.
3. Discuss facts, not rumors.
4. Define future expectations for the employee.
5. Develop timeline for correction and consequences.

When you discipline your employee, be sure you tell them how you desire that they ultimately become a valuable employee. Hebrews 12:11 teaches, "No discipline seems pleasant at the time, but painful. Later on, however, it produces a harvest of righteousness and peace for those who have been trained by it."

As a manager, you owe it to your employees to address the problem immediately rather than ignore or dismiss a problem. And address it directly with the employee, not as a generic issue in a staff meeting; everyone knows who you're talking about and will lose respect for you, the weak manager. Ultimately, you'll have greater success addressing issues and disciplining employees if you treat them as you would want to be treated.

Phase 7: Dismissing employees

Dismissing an employee hurts. If you value and respect people, letting someone go will be one of the toughest jobs you will ever perform. In order to make sure they leave with dignity, the entire process should be well thought out, prayed over, and handled delicately.

Of course, dismissing an employee should be the last straw after all the proactive approaches—good hiring, training, and coaching—have been exhausted. Even when you *are* proactive, there will be times when dismissal is warranted or necessary for the business. So how do you plan for the dismissal?

Decision-making process for dismissing employees

Is the dismissal for performance reasons? If yes, follow Matthew 18's biblical discipline model first. If no, pray for God to carefully direct your steps.

A. Look for creative solutions
   o Non-payroll expense cuts
   o Job-sharing opportunities
   o Consider full-time to part-time conversions
   o Consider across-the-board pay cuts
B. Remember the Golden Rule for severance, timing and place

Sometimes managers keep people on when they shouldn't because they don't want to be disliked. Many times, someone needs to be dismissed due to slothfulness or because they're simply in the wrong position, but true compassion requires you to do what is best for that person, even if they don't recognize or understand it at the time. God does this to us all the time. We think we need or want something, but he knows we need to experience difficulties in order to grow or enjoy his forthcoming blessing.

When I was a young CPA for a public accounting firm, I realized I didn't like the day-to-day grind of that profession. I was getting sloppy on the details, and I no longer had much drive or passion for that type of work. I was looking for a way out, but I was too apathetic to look for something else.

When the firm lost one of its largest accounts and had to cut expenses, they let me go. I immediately felt relieved, like a big burden had just been lifted. Many problem employees are looking for someone to force them to go find something they really enjoy and in which they will excel.

When it's time to dismiss, have a gentle but firm discussion, recognizing that each person handles emotions differently. Try to pick a time that will allow the employee to pack their belongings quietly. Recognize that there will need to be a way for them to say good-bye to others with whom they work. Consider the effect of any holidays or events in their life, which may cause it to be a bad time for dismissal.

Most of all, put yourself in their place. Think about their family, their unique issues with which they will have to deal, and make it as easy as possible for them. Consider risks to the security of the business and to other employees in case this person overreacts. Try to give them all of the details about money due them, future references, healthcare, and any issues that will be of concern to them such as future employment possibilities.

Dismissal is also very difficult for managers, so prepare yourself mentally and emotionally. Bathe the whole situation in prayer, and let the Lord lead you through the process. Consider all sides of the issue, the business, other employees, and the employee being dismissed. Most of all, try to plan it so that it is handled properly, professionally, and with great compassion and empathy to all parties involved.

Summary

God desires you to cherish those people who have been entrusted to your care. As much as it is within your power, you want those who work for your organization to have a pleasing experience. Jesus summarized good hiring and management practices well in Luke 6:31: "Do to others as you would have them do to you."

CHAPTER EIGHT
Shaping Your Culture

"If one part suffers, every part suffers with it;
if one part is honored, every part rejoices with it."
1 Corinthians 12:26

UCLA coaching legend John Wooden once said, "Each of us must make the effort to contribute to the best of our ability according to our individual talents. And then we put all the individual talents together for the highest good of the group… understanding that the good of the group comes first and is fundamental to being a highly productive member of a team."

Coach Wooden was famous for being able to win championships—ten in twelve years—through building a strong team rather than relying on individual stars. Although he certainly had some stars on his teams at times, the team always came first.

Likewise, Nehemiah realized that he could have set up individuals or families to build sections of the wall, but what was more effective was to make each team and their segment of the wall interlock with the team next to them. This created unity and a team effort to accomplish the overall goal, rather than individuals stealing the spotlight.

In business, the most effective organizations are ones that have built a cohesive team that works well together toward the vision of the organization rather than for individual glory. This requires shaping a healthy ethical culture.

What is culture?

While having lunch with a 94-year-old friend, I mentioned that we were doing some consulting around shaping culture in business. He looked very puzzled as he asked, "Why would *Integrity Resource Center* care about things like theater and the arts?" It was then I realized how much the word "culture" has changed over the years. What used to be considered an interest in the arts and other expressions of creativity has now evolved into a term that many use in the business community to explain how it feels to be part of a particular organization. Essentially, it is the sum of attitudes, customs, beliefs, and behaviors that distinguishes one group of people from another.

Although team members have their own attitudes, beliefs, and behaviors they bring to an organization, when you combine all of those from each team member, collectively it becomes a stew-like organism that results in your own organizational culture.

Every organization has a culture. It's up to you to decide if you choose to shape that culture *proactively* into one of which you are proud, or you *react* to the different personalities and challenges that come your way, resulting in a culture of which you may be ashamed.

Why is culture important?

In 2012, LRN Consulting performed a fascinating study called the HOW Report. Over 36,000 people in eighteen countries were surveyed about what differentiates high-performing businesses from other less-effective organizations. They discovered the organizations they were researching could be lumped into three types of cultures.

They labeled the first group "*Blind Obedience.*" These organizations had a very top-down and coercive culture. They were very dictatorial.

The second group was labeled "*Informed Acquiescence.*" These rules-based businesses had hierarchy and structure, but were not as dictatorial as the Blind Obedience category.

The last group was labeled "Self Governance." These organizations were short on policies, procedures, and rules; instead, they had a trusting environment that allowed employees to make decisions on their own. The reason for this was because their culture was strong on communicating purpose and values to team members. Decisions were made according to what would best help the organization fulfill its values and purpose, not according to a policy or rule book.

The bottom-line insight from this study was that only 3 percent of all the organizations reviewed fell into the "Self Governance" category, yet those companies had the highest performance metrics and results of any companies reviewed. By having a healthy culture that effectively trained and communicated the values and purpose of the organization, they were able to trust their team members to make decisions in the best interest of the organization. This culture of trust resulted in much higher performance and effectiveness than either the "Informed Acquiescence" or "Blind Obedience" companies.

Multiple studies I have reviewed over the years have concluded with similar findings. Culture matters, and when it is proactively shaped around the vision, mission, and values of an organization, it brings bottom-line results while also providing employees with a place to work that has purpose and meaning.

The seven drivers of culture

Now that we better understand the benefits of a healthy culture, we need to *identify* the elements that drive us towards developing a culture of which our entire team might be proud. My friend, Jerry Haney, author of *Making Culture Pay*, has developed the following seven drivers of a positive culture:

1. Vision
2. Values
3. Products and services

4. Structure/style
5. People
6. Metrics
7. Rewards/recognition

Vision

Team members want to know why they are doing what they are doing. Without understanding the organization's vision, it is difficult for an employee to connect their task to the purpose. In their mind, this can make the task feel less important and maybe even not worth doing.

Proverbs 29:18 teaches, "Where there is no vision, the people are unrestrained." Without clarity of where you are trying to take the organization, your team members are likely to carry out their tasks half-heartedly and not always in alignment with where you might hope. When vision is clear, your entire team can begin to more effectively pick and choose their priorities and be more passionate about the duties that will likely get the organization to its vision faster.

Values

Values drive behavior. If you want your team to behave in a certain way, then they need to know what you value. In today's world, you cannot assume that each team member knows right from wrong. Their past and their upbringing increasingly may not reflect values that you would be proud to have in your business.

Defining three to five core organizational values, and then communicating them effectively, will help you shape your culture in alignment with values that are pleasing to God. In Psalm 119:100, the psalmist says, "Because I have observed your precepts. I have restrained my feet from every evil way."

The right values properly communicated can help your business from straying into "every evil way."

Products and services

Your business will not exist for long if you are not providing excellent products and services. Your customer is the lifeblood of your organization, and they expect you to meet and exceed their expectations or they will move on to another product or service.

The culture of an organization is impacted dramatically by its products and services. If you are selling poor quality products, your team will become discouraged and lack enthusiasm for helping to advance the organizational vision. For those of us who desire to please God in all that we do, the bar is raised even higher. The Apostle Paul wrote in Colossians 3:23, "Whatever you do, do your work heartily, as for the Lord rather than for men." Doing our work as if we were serving Jesus only will please your customers and make your team proud.

Structure/Style

Many businesses start in a reactive mode, taking care of the needs of their customers with very little structure. Usually, policies and procedures are lacking, as well as organization. As a business matures, it realizes that some forethought and order will be needed to help carry out day-to-day duties. Procedure manuals become more important as team members are added.

For growth to be sustainable, it becomes necessary to develop organizational charts, roles and responsibilities, and clear policies and procedures. If you desire a healthy culture that doesn't overwhelm you, you need to begin thinking and applying structure and style to your organization sooner rather than later.

People

The most important part of your culture is your people. A poor job of hiring negatively impacts your culture. Even if you hire the right people, but manage them poorly, it can devastate your culture. People want to work in an environment that is safe, fair, and just. Colossians 4:1 teaches, "Masters, grant to your slaves justice and fairness, knowing that you too have a Master in heaven."

A friend recently sold his business to a much larger organization. They asked him to remain as president, which he did for a season. The culture of his business had been very family oriented, but he was dismayed to learn that the new owners of his business viewed people simply as tools to be discarded when it didn't meet their bottom-line objectives. The culture quickly turned into a dog-eat-dog environment that he could no longer tolerate.

If you follow the guidelines and principles taught in the previous chapters on servant leadership and managing people, it will help you build your team on a biblical foundation that serves your culture well.

Metrics

Many businesses are run by sales people or technicians, so sometimes there's a gap when it comes to managing the financial aspects of the organization, or in tracking measurable results.

Jesus taught in Luke 14:28, "Suppose one of you wants to build a tower. Won't you first sit down and estimate the cost to see if you have enough money to complete it?" Tracking the most important indicators for your business, including your financial indicators, is also critical for a healthy culture. If you don't have targeted goals or financial projections, it's hard to determine if you have been successful. Without proper metrics, your team will never know if they are winning or losing. They need to know how they are doing and so do you.

Rewards/Recognition

One of the most successful business stories in our community was a pharmaceutical company called Marion Laboratories. They were famous for being generous with their staff. Everyone shared in bonuses and profit sharing. The philosophy of founder Ewing Kauffman was that if workers helped bring success, they deserved to share in the rewards of that success.

When Marion Laboratories eventually sold, they had the highest sales and profit per employee of any in their industry. The company sold for billions of dollars and made hundreds of people within the company millionaires. Many believe a big part of the company's success was their profit-sharing arrangement and their quarterly employee meetings where they recognized employees for their accomplishments.

In 1 Corinthians 9:10, Paul teaches, "Whoever plows and threshes should be able to do so in the hope of sharing in the harvest." Many people may start generous bonus or profit-sharing plans, but the minute they see someone receiving as much money as top leadership, the plans often get scrapped. If you want a strong healthy culture, plan to reward and recognize those who help you succeed, and then stick with it.

How to create a healthy ethical culture

Shaping a healthy ethical culture requires thought and action. You can just react to your day-to-day circumstances and have a culture, but it's unlikely to be the culture you really want. Instead, if you desire to please God with your organization, you will want to consider the following steps.

Step 1: Assess the strength of your culture drivers

It's important to know the strength of your existing culture so you know how much work must get done in order to get the culture to where you desire. By reviewing each of the seven drivers listed above, you can begin to get a feel for the gaps and strengths in your existing culture.

At *Integrity Resource Center*, we use a tool that's designed to anonymously assess your team members' views on each of the seven drivers. This tool results in a score for each segment as compared to the norm so that gaps can be identified. Whether or not you use our tool, you need to find out what your team thinks about each of the drivers because studies show that organizational leaders have a significantly distorted view on the business when compared to their team members.

Step 2: Cast vision for the future culture

Just like sharing with the people on your team your vision for the organization, it's also helpful to give some thought as to what your vision might be for your business' culture in the future. Pondering each of the seven drivers listed above and what excellence might look like for each one can be an exercise that helps shape the culture of your organization. Putting this on paper and communicating it to your team can help guide your culture towards that vision.

Step 3: Develop your strategy and tactics

Once you have an idea as to your seven driver gaps and what you desire your future culture to look like, it's time to determine the most effective strategy to get you there. Simply setting a goal for each major item and then breaking it down to the individual tactics necessary to accomplish that goal will help you move forward. However, it's important to assign someone to be responsible for each tactic and its timeline to be achieved.

Step 4: Communicate, communicate, communicate

For many businesses, one of the biggest issues is poor communication. Too many plans and practices are communicated once then forgotten, which results in a lot of frustration for everyone who worked hard on the project. This is especially true of culture, which is a journey, not a destination. Every person you bring on board can destroy or add to the culture and reputation of your entire organization.

Your team needs to know that you are committed to this journey. You need to regularly and consistently communicate the values you want them to model. Then you need to communicate your affirmation when you find people who are doing it right. Likewise, you need to communicate when someone goes off track so they know their actions were not in alignment with the desired culture of the organization.

A friend who sold his business impressed me with the culture of his organization before the sale and how that culture continued after the sale. I was curious what he'd learned over the years of running his business, so he shared with me that the business had done okay for years, but during the last three to four of his ownership, he became dogmatically focused on communicating vision, mission, and values to each and every team member in multiple ways and on a regular basis. Being focused on culture is what took his business from "okay" to being very profitable and effective.

If you desire for your team to take seriously your efforts of shaping a healthy ethical culture, I recommend you communicate, communicate, communicate.

Step 5: Make periodic assessments and adjustments

Since shaping culture is a journey, not a destination, it's important that you periodically pause and assess your progress. You could use our seven-driver tool or just go back to your staff and subjectively assess each of the seven drivers with your team. Look for those areas in which you have improved and for those areas that still seem to have significant gaps.

Once you have reassessed the drivers, prioritize which gaps are most important to address, and then begin making the necessary course adjustments to get your culture on track with your desired vision for the future.

Summary

The way employees behave is the key indicator of your organization's culture. It not only shapes your culture, it shapes your reputation. Many studies have verified the value of a strong culture. If you desire a business that is healthy, ethical, and known for its reputation, become proactive in addressing your culture. It will enhance your bottom line, reflect well on your reputation, and your good stewardship will please God!

FOURTH KEY:

GROWING THE TOP LINE

Chapter Nine
Marketing with Truth and Love

"An honest witness does not deceive,
but a false witness pours out lies."
Proverbs 14:5

Marketing fraud is a much bigger problem than many might realize. In the pharmaceutical industry alone, there have been more than $10 billion in fines doled out by the U.S. government to well-known companies like GlaxoSmithKline and Pfizer, just between 2009 and 2013. Typically, these fines were levied for making false claims about their products.

Imagine the arrogance of Fortune 500 companies making claims to the world that their products were safe and approved by the FDA when they knew they weren't. Although it can be easy for us to cast stones at the large companies and the frauds they might commit, the reality is that many small businesses also find ways to deceive or lie to their customers for the sake of increased profit. Men and women who desire to do business God's way have to be thoughtful and careful about our marketing practices.

Marketing from God's perspective

Marketing is defined by the Merriam-Webster dictionary as "activities that are involved in making people aware of a company's products, making sure that the products are available to be bought, etc." A more biblical definition of marketing might be *"truthful* activities that are involved in making people aware of a company's products, making sure that the products are available to be bought, etc., *without any deception or harm to others."*

> *A more biblical definition of marketing might be "The truthful activities that are involved in making people aware of a company's products, making sure that the products are available to be bought, etc. without any deception or harm to others.*

Nehemiah wasn't marketing a product, but he was marketing a dream. He realized that his dream could not be fulfilled unless he communicated the vision clearly, but he also needed to communicate the truth of the current situation.

If you desire to please God through your business, your marketing should be done with truth and love. There are at least four marketing challenges that can prevent us from accomplishing that lofty goal.

Four marketing challenges
Pricing

Since the beginning of business transactions, many businessmen and women have been tempted to get ahead with deceptive or dishonest pricing. Sometimes it's unfair pricing that gives preferential treatment to those who are armed with knowledge, while taking advantage of those who don't know any better. Other times it might be price fixing with your competitors. Either way, Proverbs 11:1 teaches: "The Lord detests dishonest scales, but accurate weights find favor with him." When examining your pricing structure, consider how you would want your own mother to be treated if she were buying your products or services.

Quality

Some people have the difficult job of selling poor quality products. This can lead them to exaggerate the benefits of the product to customers or even outright lie in order to close the sale. If your product needs to be fixed, fix it! Proverbs 22:29 teaches: "Do you see someone skilled in their work? They will serve before kings; they will not serve before officials of low rank." Refine the quality of your products and services, and you will typically have plenty of opportunity to grow a profitable business.

Purity

Sex may sell product, but should it be a tool that you use in your business? The Apostle Paul taught in Ephesians 5:3, "But among you there must not be even a hint of sexual immorality, or of any kind of impurity, or of greed, because these are improper for God's holy people." The Chris Craft boat company took this directive seriously, and even though sex is often used to sell recreational products, they have established a policy and practice of modeling purity in all of their advertisements.

Sponsoring sin

Many companies use television, radio, or print advertising to promote their products. This can lead to underwriting programming that may entice others to sin. Jesus said to his disciples in Luke 17:1, "Things that cause people to stumble are bound to come, but woe to anyone through whom they come." Carefully select what programs or activities your advertising dollars sponsor.

Seven marketing plan questions

Many of you reading this book are probably much better marketers than I will ever be, so rather than waste your time on marketing strategy and tactics, I thought it would be more helpful to look at the right questions to ask when planning your marketing.

In order to develop the best marketing plan for your business, the well-known marketing guru, Seth Godin, recommends asking the following questions:

1. Who are you trying to reach?
2. What are you selling?
3. What do your prospective customers want?
4. When are your customers most likely to buy?
5. Where are the best places to reach your customer?
6. Why should your customers buy your product or service?
7. How do your customers buy your product or service?

Who are you trying to reach?

Many people desire sales so much they think everyone should be their customer. This is not a good marketing strategy. If you are not very clear on who you are serving, your customer won't be clear either. Even Jesus knew he had been sent to seek and save the lost Jews. He did not focus on trying to sell his message to Gentiles.

What are you selling?

Is your product or service simple and clear to understand? Do you have the right message to clearly communicate what you want your customer to buy? What story are you spreading? Jesus stated and restated his message clearly and consistently so there was no doubt what he expected of his followers.

What do your prospective customers want?

Although technology has allowed many products to be developed that customers could not possibly know they might want or desire, your customers usually know what they are looking for, and so you should know what they're seeking. Market research or testing a lean version of your product can be extremely valuable in determining what your customers desire and what they will buy.

Jesus knew that people ultimately were looking for eternal peace because he knew their heart. The best way to know what our customers need or want is to ask them.

When are your customers most likely to buy?

What events in the customer's life might trigger their desire to purchase your product or service? What is their point of pain or need? How do you make sure they know about your product at those moments in their life? Jesus frequently met people at their point of pain; when they were sick, grieving, or when life seemed empty. It will help us be better marketers if we will learn when our customers typically have pain relative to our product or service.

Where are the best places to reach your customers?

Not only does this speak to your customers' buying habits, but also to distribution. Will your customers most likely buy online, in a retail store, from a wholesaler, or from a face-to-face interaction with a salesperson? What needs to be in place for a customer to take action when they are in the right place?

Jesus knew that if he only delivered his message in the synagogues, he would miss the majority of the people he desired to reach. He went into the marketplace and different communities and villages so he could reach as many people as possible.

Why should your customers buy your product or service?

It's critical that you know why your customers buy your product or service. Are they buying only because of price, or is it due to quality, convenience, or other factors you need to consider. What do your customers tell their friends about your product? You need to know your "value proposition." What value are you adding to a customer's life and how much do they have to pay to receive that value? Is the value proposition strong enough for them to come back and tell others about your product or service?

Jesus had a tremendous value proposition. He was offering eternal life, and the only cost was submission and belief in him as the son of God. But even with that tremendous value, not everyone was willing to buy. You also need to realize why people may not buy from you so that you focus your time on those who will buy. That's why Jesus spent more time with sinners than he did Pharisees.

How do your customers buy your product or service?

A significant amount of business is now done online. If your process is cumbersome or requires too much customer information, your customer may never complete the order. This question also speaks to the issue of how customers will become aware of your offer and whether it's easy for them to respond at that moment. Many businesses talk about their product's features and benefits, but forget to ask for the order. Make sure that wherever and whenever your customers encounter your product or service, they know how to follow through and purchase what you have to offer.

Jesus shared with the disciples how to make new disciples. He modeled for them how to share the Gospel, how to ask people to commit to follow him, and how to be baptized and filled with the Holy Spirit so that they might live an eternal life with our Lord and Savior.

Summary

Many business owners stumble in their faith in the pursuit of more sales and profit. Marketing is a critical factor of business, but don't let it be a snare to you modeling your faith to others. Develop a marketing plan for your business using the above seven questions, and be sure that you weave in—and ground your plans with—truth and love. God desires for you to do business his way. You can succeed *and* flourish without lying, cheating, deceiving, or harming others!

CHAPTER TEN
Growing Sales God's Way

"A good name is more desirable than great riches;
to be esteemed is better than silver or gold."
Proverbs 22:1

Scott was a recent college graduate in a management training program when I first met him. He had a plan to own his own company and a Mercedes by the time he was thirty. Every day he pinched pennies in incredible ways to work toward his goals.

After thirty years of watching Scott's career from afar, I witnessed a person who achieved many of his financial goals, but who destroyed many relationships—including his marriage and family—in the meantime. Even selling his business for millions of dollars was not enough for him. He tried to leverage his wealth for even greater returns, which eventually resulted in multiple business failures and being prosecuted by the government for fraud, and then banned from the industry in which he worked. Scott esteemed riches more than his reputation.

Growth for the sake of growth and added wealth is a risk for many who are otherwise talented salespeople. In this chapter we will define sales, contrast the world's view on sales with God's view, and then reveal the benefits and pathway to growing sales God's way.

Sales

Sales is often described as "the exchange of goods or services for money." Since there is a buyer and a seller involved in any transaction, it requires the price and terms to be mutually beneficial to each party, or one or the other of the parties will refuse to participate. The problem arises when there is an *appearance* of value on both sides that lasts long enough for a transaction to happen once.

If, after the transaction is complete, one of the parties discovers new information (like a shoddy product or that the price was higher than the competition), it can result in ill feelings. This can turn a business relationship into a one-time transaction that may have benefitted the seller temporarily, but harms them in the long term.

Many people in the sales world get so focused on the short-term transaction—commissions, bonuses or other incentives—that they overlook the value of a long-term relationship and the good reputation that can ensue.

Many salespeople may think that added money in the pocket today is worth the risk of losing a customer long-term, but God is all about relationships. He desires us to sell products and services that adds value to the lives of others, and strengthens relationships rather than tears them down.

Following God's approach to sales brings many benefits, including:
- *Longer term customers and relationships*
- *Peace of mind*
- *Better reputation*
- *Less legal and moral challenges*

How to sell God's way

The Golden Rule of "doing unto others as you would have them do unto you" is a great starting point for selling God's way. Nobody likes feeling like they have been cheated or fleeced. Trust is the underpinning of all commerce. Without trust, it's difficult to know if a price is fair. Without trust, it's impossible to know if the promises made before the sale will be kept.

Fortunately, Jesus was the master of building trust. We can learn a great deal about building trust from examining the way he went about building his team of disciples. For the sake of simplicity and to make it easy to remember, I am going to use the acronym **TRUST** to describe how Jesus sold his disciples on giving up their careers to follow him.

The Matthew 4 account of Jesus calling his disciples seems oversimplified at first. Verse 19 says, "'Come, follow me,' Jesus said, 'and I will make you fishers of men.' At once they left their nets and followed him."

It didn't make sense to me that Peter and Andrew would cash it all in and follow Jesus just because he asked. This led me to study the accounts of this story in each of the four gospels. Suddenly the picture became clearer.

The first "T" in TRUST stands for testimonials of others. I discovered from the book of John that Peter and Andrew were disciples of John the Baptist. John gave testimony to Jesus being the Messiah when he told Peter and Andrew, "There goes the Lamb of God."

To forge a new relationship, we sometimes need the testimony of someone who knows us and/or our work. It's common to see testimonials used to leverage another person's relationship with someone whom you would like to do business.

Even Nehemiah understood the value of leveraging others when he chose the head priest to build the first section of the wall. The priest in that day was the power broker. By leading with the priests, Nehemiah was able to leverage their relational capital to lend credibility to his project.

The "R" in TRUST stands for relationships. After John pointed Peter and Andrew towards the Messiah, we learn they spent time with Jesus. This began the important work of knitting their hearts with his, allowing them to realize that Jesus cared about them. In sales, people will not typically trust you or show loyalty until they know that you care. There's no substitute for time spent in relationship with others.

The "U" in TRUST stands for under promising and over performing. In Luke's account of Jesus calling Peter and Andrew to follow him, we learn that Jesus first amazes Peter and Andrew by telling them to let down their nets for a catch. He didn't promise that he was going to fill their boats with fish. The professional fishermen had fished that lake all night long without catching so much as a minnow. Peter's and Andrew's expectations were very low. It's no wonder that Peter fell in repentance before Jesus after seeing his power. After obeying Jesus, the two fishing boats were so full of fish that they almost sunk.

We should strive to only make promises to our customers we can keep. We also can amaze others when we provide far more than what they expected. Trust follows exceeded expectations.

The "S" in TRUST stands for serve. When we serve others at their point of need, it goes a long way towards winning their favor and trust. Jesus knew that Peter and Andrew were frustrated. They had fished all night without any success. These were skilled fishermen who had worked long and hard with no tangible results. Jesus knew the best way to serve Peter and Andrew was to provide for their needs in a way they could appreciate.

Two boatfuls of fish brought these men into a humble state willing to give up all they had to follow the man who cared enough to meet their needs. If you look for ways to best serve your customer or prospects, it will build trust in a way that will win customers and allow you to build a solid base of sales for your organization.

The last "T" in TRUST represents telling the truth. Jesus preached from the boat of Peter and Andrew, sharing the truth of the gospel. If Jesus had lied or stretched the truth in any way during his teaching time, it would have undermined everything else he said or did. His telling the truth enabled him to build greater trust in his relationship with his disciples.

It's tempting to stretch the truth in order to sell more product. Don't succumb to the temptation. It will undermine your reputation and ultimately result in less sales rather than more.

Jesus built trust with these two disciples, which resulted in their willingness to walk away from their fishing enterprise, their boats, their nets, and even more amazing, two entire boats filled with fish they could have easily sold for income. Jesus, the ultimate salesperson, built the largest sales organization in history. It has spanned more than two thousand years and millions of people. Building trust in your sales efforts will serve you well.

Summary

Many people become so focused on the short-term benefits of the sales transaction that they sacrifice the relationship and the long-term benefits that result from those relationships. In order to grow your sales God's way, people need to be an important part of the equation. Building trust with others is critical for long-term gain and an ongoing strong customer base.

Fortunately, Jesus modeled for us some great approaches to building trust. If we leverage the "Testimonials" of others, build lasting "Relationships," "Under promise and over perform," "Serve" others and are "Truth" tellers, we have a much higher likelihood of success.

FIFTH KEY:

ENHANCING THE BOTTOM LINE

CHAPTER ELEVEN
Seven Keys to Financial Success

"His master replied, 'Well done, good and faithful servant!
You have been faithful with a few things:
I will put you in charge of many things.
Come and share your master's happiness!'"
Matthew 25:21

In 1946, Truett Cathy and his brother opened his first restaurant. Many who look at the success of Chick-fil-A® and their 1800 plus stores may think it has become an "overnight success." But it took twenty years of perseverance and faithfulness for Truett to even brand and open the first Chick-fil-A® store.

During those first twenty years, Truett had two restaurants burn to the ground. He tried to license his secret chicken recipe to others before realizing this was a mistake. And he competed with stores that were open seven days a week, while he held to his conviction of being closed on Sundays.

Although he was a restaurant operator and not a financial guru, over the course of Truett's life, he surrounded himself with people who helped him steward the stores to become one of the most financially successful restaurant chains in the country. Truett modeled well the stated purpose of Chick-fil-A®: "To glorify God by being a faithful steward of all that is entrusted to us. To have a positive influence on all who come in contact with Chick-fil-A."

Many people in business may be good salespeople or technicians, but not well versed on finances. In order to be a long-term faithful steward of your business, it's critical that you gain at least a basic understanding of finances. Without a basic understanding of your financial condition, you can't properly "count the cost" of what your cash needs might be in the future.

Nehemiah gave much thought and consideration to his desire to rebuild the walls of Jerusalem. He was so well prepared that when the king asked him what he needed, Nehemiah didn't hesitate. He had a list of all the resources necessary at the ready. Since he was prepared to answer when he was asked, God gave him favor with the king and the king agreed to provide all that Nehemiah needed.

This chapter is designed to give you an understanding of the basics of business finance, as well as an overview of seven keys to financial success.

Financial statement basics

Proverbs 27:23–24 provides some great wisdom: "Be sure you know the condition of your flocks, give careful attention to your herds; for riches do not endure forever, and a crown is not secure for all generations." Financial statements are one of the best tools for helping you discover the true condition of your business.

Unfortunately, many small businesses never see any financial information until they are handed a tax return to sign long after their year-end has been completed. This is far too late to make necessary adjustments that will maximize profitability.

Audited financial statements contain many different reports and footnotes, but the basic two statements with which you need to become familiar are the **income statement** and the **balance sheet**. Let's begin with the income statement, which is sometimes known as the profit and loss statement

Income statement

This statement reveals the revenues, cost of goods sold, operating expenses, and ultimate net-profit of the organization over a defined period of time. Whether it is monthly or annual, an income statement helps you determine the level of financial activity your business experienced during that period of time. Many people look at the gross revenue and then at the net profit, and ignore the rest. You will discover why this is short sighted as we discuss the seven keys to financial success later in this chapter.

Balance sheet

The balance sheet is by far the most overlooked financial document, yet it is usually the first thing your bank wants to see. The balance sheet is simply a document that examines a moment in time for your business.

The "as of" date on the balance sheet provides you with a list and value of the asset categories your business owns at that moment. It also lists the various liabilities or financial obligations you owe to others, and finally, it shows the net of those two numbers so you can see the net worth or owner's equity in the business.

The value of this information is so you can clearly see what would be left after you paid off all debts, if you had to liquidate today. Many people are so focused on cash flow and what is in the checkbook that they overlook how much cash is tied up in outstanding accounts receivable (monies that you have billed other people).

There also can be a significant amount of cash tied up in inventory. Without reviewing your balance sheet occasionally, you can also deceive yourself on how much debt is outstanding to your vendors and lenders.

Profit versus cash flow

The first business I ever owned was a car rental agency. After getting the doors open and conducting business for a couple of months, I anxiously compiled my income statement. I will never forget the pride I felt as I totaled the numbers and revealed a very small profit for the first time. However, my pride was quickly dashed when I opened my checkbook and realized I had no cash.

Many people assume that cash flow and profit are the same, but because of the balance sheet and non-cash items like inventory and accounts receivable, they can be vastly different. My business was showing a profit, but because I had spent money on inventory, I had no cash.

Accrual-based statements compile *all* of your assets and liabilities, like your inventory and monies you owe your vendors. A cash-based statement ignores those until they turn into cash. If you are not receiving accrual-based financial statements, you are not seeing the total picture. Many businesses pay taxes on a cash basis, so they never see an accrual-based set of financial statements, which distorts the true financial picture of the business.

Accurate financial statements are crucial for you to properly manage your business. Ask your accountant to provide you with accrual-based financial statements on a monthly basis. It will be some of the best money you spend because it will give you a glimpse into what's really happening in your business financially.

Seven keys to financial success

Most of the entrepreneurs I worked with in my former consulting practice were not very familiar with the financial side of their business. Knowing that I could not expect these people to become accountants or chief financial officers, I broke down the seven most important financial indicators I felt they needed to know:

1. Sales growth

2. Gross profit margin
3. Overhead margin
4. Return on equity
5. Generosity factor
6. Leverage ratio
7. Turnover ratios

Sales growth

There are many myths that business leaders buy into, including the belief that "more sales is always better." This philosophy can have disastrous consequences.

When I was a commercial lender, I had a loan customer who was growing his specialty advertising business very rapidly. He had borrowed a great deal of money with the promise that he would pay off his line of credit the following year from his sales growth.

The following year arrived, his debt was at its highest level, and he wanted us to significantly increase his line of credit. Due to his rapid sales growth, the amount his customers owed him was growing so fast that it was consuming all of his working capital. His answer to my concerns was that he intended to ramp up sales even more. Even though I produced a cash-flow projection for him that revealed his company would be broke if he didn't slow down his sales growth, he chose to push ahead.

Proverbs 21:5 teaches, "The plans of the diligent lead to profit as surely as haste leads to poverty." Sales growth is great if you have strong margins and can collect your customer's money quickly enough to fund your cash flow needs. However, *steady growth* is what's required for most businesses.

For those of you who desire to track these seven keys, I have simple formulas for you or your accountant to use on a regular basis. *The sales growth formula is: (this year's sales minus last year's sales) divided by last year's sales equals your sales growth percentage.*

For example, if your sales were $1.2 million this year, and $1 million last year, your sales growth would be ($1,200,000 - $1,000,000) / $1,000,000 = 20%. Comparing your actual growth to your budgeted growth will help you determine if you are growing faster or slower than desired.

Gross profit margin

Randy had a home remodeling business that wasn't as profitable as he thought it should be when he hired me to do some consulting work for him. When I examined his financial statements and looked at his industry standards at that time, I discovered that Randy's gross profit margin was far below his industry average.

His peers were averaging a 40 percent markup in profit over their direct material and labor costs while Randy was at less than 30 percent. By helping him better understand industry averages, we were able to help him price his services at a much higher rate, eventually exceeding the industry average of 40 percent, and making his business significantly more profitable.

Some service industries will not have a gross profit margin to monitor, although many could do a better job of tracking their direct job costs. Gross profit margin is the difference between your revenue on a job and the direct material and labor expenses it requires to complete that job. Don't include your overhead expenses; just the necessary direct job costs to produce the product.

The formula for tracking gross profit margin is: (revenue minus cost of goods or services sold) divided by revenue equals your gross profit margin percentage. This gives you a percentage to compare to your industry or your prior history. For example, if Randy had a $100,000 remodeling project for which the labor and materials cost him $70,000, then he has a gross profit of $30,000. This $30,000 divided by his revenue of $100,000 gives him a 30 percent gross profit margin. ($100,000 - $30,000) / $100,000 = 30%.

If he knows that the industry standard is 40 percent, then he can quickly discover that he could have improved his profit by $10,000 if he had priced his services according to industry standards.

Overhead margin

The expenses for your business include your cost of goods or services sold and your operating expenses. The operating expenses are usually considered to be your overhead. For a business to be efficient, you need for your operating expenses to run very lean. Expenses like your rent, phones, office supplies, etc., are operating expenses that can creep up, especially during good times.

A friend was running a construction business when the economy collapsed in 2008. He shared with me that times had been so good for so long prior to 2008 that they had gotten sloppy. Their overhead had increased dramatically without really adding value to the bottom line.

When the work stopped coming in the way it previously had, he begin slashing expenses. In only a year he realized that even though his revenue had decreased 40 percent, he was actually making more bottom-line profit because of the wasted operating expense he was able to trim.

Overhead margin is calculated by: (total operating expense/sales.) This equals the percentage of every sales dollar being spent on overhead. For instance, a 30 percent overhead margin means that for every dollar in sales created, you are spending $.30 of that dollar on overhead. For a well-run business, it's important this percentage be as low as possible.

The Apostle Paul wrote in 1 Corinthians 4:2, "Now it is required that those who have been given a trust must prove faithful." Managing your overhead is critical if you want to prove faithful in your business.

Return on equity

Many people believe their business is simply a job, but a business is an investment. Just like you would invest some of your excess capital in a mutual fund or another form of investment, you deserve a return on the monies invested in your business. Furthermore, God desires you to make a good return on *his* money. Jesus taught in Luke 12:48, "From everyone who has been given much, much will be demanded; and from the one who has been entrusted with much, much more will be asked."

The best way to determine if you're having a successful return on investment is to analyze it the way you would your personal investments. This would best be described as return on equity. *The formula for return on equity is: net profit after tax divided by owner's equity or net worth on your Balance Sheet equals the percentage of return on equity.* This percentage can then be compared to your other investments.

For instance, if your business had a $100,000 profit last year and your balance sheet claims you had $500,000 in net worth or owner's equity at year end, your return on equity would be 20 percent. $100,000 / $500,000 = 20%.

Generosity factor

We will be discussing generosity later in this book, however, if you desire to know how generous you were from your business last year, you should compare the level of giving you did from your business relative to your bottom-line profit. *The formula for* the *generosity factor would be: charitable giving divided by net profit before tax equals your percentage of generosity.* If you wish to tithe (10 percent) from your net profit, then the result of the generosity factor should be 10 percent or more.

For instance, if you earned $100,000 before tax last year, then 10 percent of that would be $10,000. If you followed through and gave $10,000 to charitable activities, you would see your generosity factor calculated like this: $10,000 / $100,000 = 10%. Some people may choose to give from their gross revenue. If so, you can substitute revenue for net profit in the above formula.

Leverage ratio

As a banker for many years, one of the first things I was trained to look for when a business owner handed me their financial statements was how much leverage, or debt, the business was carrying.

The leverage ratio would quickly reveal whether the creditors or owners had more risk in the business. If I, as the banker, had more risk than the owners, it raised concern that they were getting most of the upside rewards, but we were taking most of the risk.

The leverage ratio is calculated by: total liabilities divided by owner's equity or net worth equals how much liability to equity was in the business. For example, if my business has $100,000 in total liabilities, but my net worth is only $50,000, then the resulting ratio would be 2 to 1. $100,000 / $50,000 = 2.

As a banker, this ratio tells me that the bank has two times more capital at risk than the owner. Since the owner receives any profits and the bank only earns an interest rate, the owner is receiving most of the benefits for very little of the risk. If, on the other hand, this business had $500,000 in net worth, the ratio would be 0.20 to 1. ($100,000 / $500,000). This would reveal that the owner has significantly more to lose than the lender.

One of the myths in business is that it's best to use other people's money to leverage for a higher return on equity. Although this may prove to be true at times, it puts your business at risk and makes it harder and more costly to obtain funding. In the next chapter we will discuss debt and its pitfalls more extensively.

Turnover ratios

In the previous balance sheet discussion, I mentioned that there are factors on the sheet that are often overlooked or not realized by simply reviewing the income statement. The most important of these are accounts receivable, inventory, and accounts payable.

These three items are only found on an accrual-based balance sheet, but are very important factors in monitoring and improving your cash flow. The best way to monitor these three factors is through what is often referred to as turnover ratios. During times of growth, it is very easy for these ratios to be overlooked to the detriment of your cash flow.

For example, if you bill your customers for the product you provide on a net 30 basis, that means you expect them to pay you within thirty days. If an average month's sales for you is $1 million, then you will likely have about $1 million in outstanding accounts receivable at any point in time, provided that all of your customers are paying you at the agreed-upon 30-day term.

However, what if the economy slows or you don't stay on top of your accounts receivable, then the average turnover grows to sixty days. This would mean, instead of $1 million in accounts receivable, you would now have $2 million in accounts receivable. Your cash flow just took a $1 million hit. Ouch!

This example can also be used for inventory. If your inventory grows and you are not managing it well, it eats into your cash flow and can cause great harm.

On the other hand, accounts payable is money you owe your vendors. Many businesses view this as free credit, and therefore, try to stretch it out as long as possible. This can run counter to your desire to please God with your business, and should be a carefully considered practice. Proverbs 3:27–28 teaches, "Do not withhold good from those to whom it is due, when it is in your power to do it. Do not say to your neighbor, go and come back, and tomorrow I will give it, when you have it with you."

The formulas for tracking these three turnover ratios are:

*Accounts receivable turnover = (accounts receivable / annual sales) * 365 days*

*Inventory turnover = (inventory / annual cost of goods sold) * 365 days*

*Accounts payable turnover = (accounts payable / cost of goods sold) * 365 days*

Summary

Being a good steward of God's business requires a basic understanding of the financial condition of the business. This may require you to hire some good financial help, but it will be worth the money and time invested. Even if you have good financial help, as the primary steward over the business, you need to grow comfortable with learning the basics in your finances.

If you simply begin tracking these seven keys to financial success on a regular basis—preferably monthly—you will begin to understand when an area is going off track. This can allow you to ask intelligent questions and determine where you need to dig deeper into the detail.

Seven Key Formulas

1. Sales growth - (this year's sales - last year's sales)/ last year's sales
2. Gross profit margin – (total sales – cost of sales)/total sales
3. Overhead margin – (total operating expense/revenue)
4. Return on equity – (net profit after tax/owner's equity)
5. Generosity factor – (charitable giving/net profit before tax)
6. Leverage ratio – (total liabilities/owner's equity)
7. Turnover ratios
   a. Accounts receivable turnover = (accounts receivable/annual sales) * 365 days
   b. Inventory turnover = (inventory/annual cost of goods sold) * 365 days
   c. Accounts payable turnover = (accounts payable/cost of goods sold) * 365 days

CHAPTER TWELVE

Crushing Debt

"Do not be one who shakes hands in pledge or puts up security for
debts; if you lack the means to pay,
your very bed will be snatched from under you."
Proverbs 22:26–27

A couple of businessmen I met years ago bought an apartment complex at a significant discount. The property was structurally sound, had great cash flow, high occupancy, and looked like a dream investment. From a banker's perspective, it looked even better when they only needed to borrow 50 percent of the purchase price.

Soon after they bought the property, they discovered the complex had an environmental problem. They had done the required environmental inspections prior to purchasing, but this was something new the Environmental Protection Agency had not previously required.

What looked like an incredible investment and an excellent loan for the bank ended up being a total loss. The apartment complex had to be leveled. Since no insurance coverage was available for this new issue, the investors were financially destroyed and the lender took a large loss.

This experience, along with many others I've witnessed in my career, has driven me to be a believer in the proverb, "Do not be one who shakes hands in pledge or puts up security for debts; if you lack the means to pay, your very bed will be snatched from under you."

Nehemiah watched his project come to a screeching halt due to the crushing impact that debt had on his team of people. Not only had they been hit by famine, but their fellow Israelites had oppressed them with debt terms and conditions that charged them high interest and even put the borrower's children in bondage. Nehemiah swiftly moved into action to release people from the crush their debt had brought on them.

Regardless of how careful we might approach debt, it has risks that can devastate us financially and undermine our faith spiritually. Fortunately, God has a better plan than the bondage that debt can bring.

Debt according to God's Word

According to the 2015 Kauffman Foundation Entrepreneurship Policy Digest, 40 percent of funding for start-up businesses comes from bank-financed debt. Earlier research from the Kauffman Foundation discovered that 54 percent of the funding for business start-ups came from some form of debt. This means that the majority of entrepreneurs have grown accustomed to depending on debt for their business ventures. But God's ways usually counter the culture, and his views on debt are no different.

> *Let me be clear, you will not find anywhere in scripture that debt is listed as a sin. However, it is often mentioned as a potential curse.*

Debt, in its simplest terms, is a presumption on the future. You are buying something today with someone else's money, with the anticipation that you will be able to pay it back later. Our bankruptcy statistics show that this presumption doesn't always work out so well. Ecclesiastes 11:2 teaches, "Give portions to seven, yes to eight, for you do not know what disaster may come upon the land." When you take on debt, you are presuming that no disaster will come upon you.

Let me be clear, you will not find anywhere in scripture that debt is listed as a sin. However, it is often mentioned as a potential curse. In Deuteronomy 28, God lists all the blessings he will provide for the Israelites if they obey his commands, including that they would be lenders, not borrowers. He goes on in that same chapter to list the curses if they disobey. Being a borrower at the mercy of creditors is one of those curses.

God's best for us is to be free of the bondage of debt. He even established a practice of lenders being required to forgive the debts of their fellow Israelites every seven years so that there was hope on the horizon of being free from bondage.

Debt often comes from a lack of faith. Hebrews 11:6 teaches, "And without faith it is impossible to please God, because anyone who comes to him must believe that he exists and that he rewards those who earnestly seek him." If we truly believe God exists, and he is calling you to start or grow a business, is it too much to believe he can provide the necessary funding for that business without saddling you with a curse?

When I owned my consulting practice, I made a commitment to build the business without debt. There came a season when God wanted me to learn a higher level of faith. New business opportunities had dried up and so had our cash.

Although the amount was very small, I had some company bills that were due and no money to pay them. Either I was going to have to borrow money, close the doors, or God was going to have to show up. I prayed fervently for a lousy $1,750, but to no avail.

On the due date of my bills, I was broken and scared, but I kneeled and committed that I would close the business that day rather than trust a lender more than God. Although this may not be what God calls you to do, he made it clear to me that I was to lead this business in faith without relying upon debt.

Later that day, a man I had never met came to my office. He informed me that he had been praying for someone to help him develop a plan for his business when he was referred to our organization. He lived in St. Louis—four hours away—but he felt God had told him to drive to Kansas City to see me, without even calling in advance!

Our organization had a set fee schedule for the kind of plan he was requesting. It was $3,500 with a 50 percent deposit up front. He wrote me a check on the spot for the $1,750 I needed. God can provide for the capital you need in any strange way he determines is best!

Seven steps to crushing your debt

As you read this chapter, you may be feeling crushed by the debt your business is already carrying. It may seem impossible at this point for you to ever become debt-free in your business, but with God, all things are possible. There are certainly consequences for our past decisions, and we cannot presume that God will give us a pass from those consequences. But we can be assured that we serve a grace-filled God who has the ability to help us become free from anything, including debt that may have us in bondage.

Before you can run a business free of debt, you must become debt free. There are only three ways to eliminate debt.

1. Sell assets and apply the proceeds to your debt.
2. Raise outside capital to pay down your debt.
3. Apply your excess cash flow to your debt.

Here are seven steps you can apply to your situation that will help you become debt free.

1. Prayer
2. Assess your current debts
3. Set a goal
4. Change your behaviors
5. Make cash flow adjustments
6. Liquidate assets
7. Develop and execute a debt repayment schedule

Prayer

God is the power source that can provide the wisdom and wealth you need to begin crushing your debt. Pray regularly and fervently, listen to his leading, and carefully obey.

Assess your current debts

Your balance sheet should provide you with the summary and totals of your different forms of debt, but many people accumulate so many different forms of debt they are not fully aware of how much they have compiled. Develop a list of each individual loan and/or credit card debt you have for your business.

List the total amount owed, the amount of each monthly payment due, the due date of each payment, and the interest rate. After you have compiled your list, sort it by the largest amount outstanding first all the way down to your smallest amount owed. It's also helpful to note the collateral on each loan so that you recognize what debts are secured and what debts have no collateral, and therefore are considered unsecured.

Set a goal

After assessing your level of debt, you need to establish a goal for paying if off. Establish an aggressive, but realistic, goal for when you desire to be debt free in your business. Having a goal is important to keep yourself motivated.

A young man I consulted with many years ago had accumulated a great deal of credit card debt in his business. It was enough debt that I thought it would take him years to recover. I was thrilled for him when he called me eight months later and proclaimed he was debt free.

When I asked him how he managed it so quickly, he said that he got angry about the debt and determined that if he would quit using independent contractors and do the work himself, he could get debt free in months instead of years. But he had to be willing to work seventy to eighty hours a week for a while. His goal drove him through those long hours to victory. Set yourself a goal, put it where you and your team can see it, and drive relentlessly towards victory!

Change your behavior

Your existing debt did not just happen. It came from your past choices and behavior. Many business leaders impulsively buy new equipment, trucks, planes, and other items. Sometimes they use credit cards or make commitments without thinking it through.

If you have credit cards in your wallet that have enabled your poor behavior—destroy them! If you have trouble buying things you shouldn't, make a written commitment to yourself and God, then give it to someone who loves you enough to hold you accountable, and give them permission to keep you on track.

Make cash flow adjustments

Improving your cash flow is the best long-term strategy to speed up the rate of debt repayment. This requires that you examine both sales and ways to increase your income, as well as your expenses. Many people assume decreasing expenses, especially payroll, is the only solution, but there may be many income-enhancing ideas your team can help identify if they are asked.

Unfortunately, when it comes to expense reduction, the biggest line item for most businesses is payroll. Consider creative ways to get the job done efficiently. You may not need to terminate staff if you look for people who can do their job in less hours. Modifying schedules, job sharing, and many other ideas may provide solutions that are win/win with your staff. Be careful, though; many businesses end up cutting staff, which may eventually drive revenue down more than the benefits that payroll cuts can bring.

Liquidate assets

When you have debt hanging over your head, every unproductive or underproductive asset should be considered something that can be sold. Maybe you have equipment that isn't being used that can be sold. Even if you don't get much for the asset, it can save money in storage, maintenance, or other related expenses.

Some businesses have been able to sell real estate and lease it back, freeing up equity to pay debt. Others should look at excess inventory that can be liquidated, or do a better job of collecting accounts receivable. Each dollar you obtain from selling unproductive assets is a dollar applied to debt and towards your goal of being debt free.

Develop and execute a debt repayment schedule

When you begin chasing your goal of becoming debt free, you need some early successes. Many people, especially those who are financially oriented, want to focus on paying off the debt with the highest interest rate first. Although this makes sense, it usually is more fruitful to experience some early success and increase your motivation by paying off smaller debts first than it is to chase interest rates.

By throwing any excess cash towards your lowest outstanding balance, you will see a debt eliminated more quickly, which will give you a sense of satisfaction and hope that you can eventually eliminate the larger debts, as well. The other benefit is that whatever you were paying monthly on that small debt can now be applied each month to the next debt you target to eliminate. As Dave Ramsey discusses, this creates a snowball of cash flow freed up to apply towards debt after debt.

Planning for the future

As you begin having some success on eliminating your debt, you will have some temptations to go back into debt. Without making a commitment, you will have seasons when you feel so optimistic that you jump right back into old habits. Impulsive spending and the use of debt are hard to stamp out without a long-term written commitment.

Commit to yourself to remain debt free, put it in writing, and place it somewhere you will not forget. You will also need some accountability. This may require that a board of directors, a spouse, a peer group, or others know of your pledge and have your permission to hold you accountable.

If you are concerned about your impulses and lack of self-control at times, you might even create a board policy and practice about what steps are necessary before any debt can be approved. At a minimum, remember that it's God's money you are spending, so shouldn't he be consulted before you pull out that credit card or sign that loan document?

I'm not naïve enough to know that each of you have bought into the dream of being completely debt free. If you have determined that you are fine with some level of risk in your business, then let me at least give you a few ideas on limiting your risk.

Limit personal guarantees. Most small businesses that borrow from a bank are required to have their principals in the business personally guarantee the company loans. This means if the company isn't able to pay, the lender will come after you personally. It's very difficult to avoid this provision, but it can be done, especially with God's help, if you are mindful of it and boldly ask your bank what it would take for them to give you some relief in this area.

Equity. One of the best ways you can limit the amount of debt is to save for future purchases. Build equity in all of your assets, including your bank account. With more equity, you run less risk of the bank seizing your assets. You can also get preferential treatment from the bank when they view the amount of equity you have in the asset being pledged, which frees them from much risk.

Cash flow margin. Some people will take on loan payments that make their ability to service the debt razor thin. When considering a loan, know how much your current monthly cash flow has been, and compare that amount to your proposed monthly loan payment. Make sure there is a large margin of cash flow for those seasons when things go wrong.

Summary

Many people in business have different levels of risk they are willing to accept. Debt can be a tool that can enhance your business returns, but it's important to remember that all debt is presuming on the future and squeezes God out of the equation. God has the ability to cover your financial needs if you allow him into the process.

Prayerfully consider what level of risk God wants you to take with his business, and then develop a plan to get your current debt to that level. Finally, make a long-term commitment to be free of bondage in the future.

CHAPTER THIRTEEN

Giving Generously

"Each man should give what he has decided in his heart to give,
not reluctantly or under compulsion,
for God loves a cheerful giver."
2 Corinthians 9:7

Bob had been faithfully giving from his paycheck for years when he attended Larry Burkett's "Business by the Book" workshop. That day he was challenged to consider that God owned his business, as well, and therefore deserved a tithe from the business. This had never occurred to Bob. It convicted him so much that he later discussed it with his brother.

Bob and his brother owned a family business that was experiencing some difficult financial challenges at that time. They were just beginning to be profitable again, but much of that cash flow was needed to pay back some debt. To begin giving from company profits seemed impossible, yet these two generous men were excited for the opportunity to give cheerfully to God's work in their community.

Today, this family business has a foundation that has generously funded millions of dollars of ministry. These men have boldly used their business to apply 2 Corinthians 9:7's admonition, "Each man should give what he has decided in his heart to give, not reluctantly or under compulsion, for God loves a cheerful giver."

Why should I give?

While working my way through college, I occasionally needed some financial help. Many times my grandmother generously stepped forward with some cash. Little did she know that I kept a journal of every gift. (I was proud of my self-sufficiency.)

After college, I saved enough money to pay her back in full. She was offended and didn't want repayment, but after my insistence, she told me to return the favor by supporting my younger brother's college expenses. I became her conduit of generosity towards my brother.

Unfortunately, for my brother, I was not as gracious as my grandmother. I couldn't resist using my gifts as a platform for my views and agenda to be expressed to my brother. Many years later my brother asked my grandmother, "Grandma, why didn't you give me money for college instead of asking Rick to help me? When you give, you do it with a smile, when Rick gave, it always came with a lecture."

God is kind of like my grandmother. He uses us to distribute his wealth to those in need. We can choose to give to his purposes and please him, or we can refuse, and risk him being less generous with us in the future. Proverbs 19:17 teaches, "He who is kind to the poor lends to the Lord, and he will reward him for what he has done."

Giving to my brother was out of obedience, but if I had given with grace and a generous spirit, it also would have been out of love. God prefers our obedience as well as our love.

Nehemiah knew the importance of generosity. He lived in an era after the Lord had punished the Israelites due to their disobedience in many different ways, including in their giving. There were several reforms that Nehemiah set in motion during his time in Jerusalem, but giving back to God from the first fruits of their crops was near the top.

There are many other good reasons why you should give to God's work. Here are three.

God commands it. Malachi 3:8–10 says, "Will a man rob God? Yet you rob me. But you ask, 'How do we rob you?'

"In tithes and offerings. You are under a curse—the whole nation of you—because you are robbing me. Bring the whole tithe into the storehouse, that there may be food in my house. Test me in this," says the Lord Almighty, "and see if I will not throw open the floodgates of heaven and pour out so much blessing that you will not have room enough for it."

God deserves it. Ecclesiastes 5:19, "Moreover, when God gives any man wealth and possessions, and enables him to enjoy them, to accept his lot and be happy in his work-this is a gift of God." Out of God's gifts to us he asks us to be generous to others.

God blesses it. Luke 6:38, "Give and it will be given to you. A good measure, pressed down, shaken together and running over, will be poured into your lap. For with the measure you use, it will be measured to you."

How much should I give?

The Old Testament's focus is primarily on tithing. The word "tithe" means "a tenth." The first scriptural reference to tithing is when Abraham gave a tenth of all of his possessions to Melchizedek, the king of Salem. It is important to note that this was prior to any commandments from God about tithing. Abraham willingly gave a tenth of his spoils to Melchizedek, who the book of Hebrews infers actually may have been God in the flesh.

Subsequent to Abraham, God commanded the Israelites to give from their work efforts a tithe to the Levites. This was a reminder that God provided the fruit of their harvest and that they should give back to him by providing for the needs of his priests and ministry leaders, the Levites.

Many people have heard a lot about the tithe, but few seem to realize that God didn't stop there with the Israelites. Depending upon how you interpret a few key passages, it is easy to make a case that the Israelites were expected to give 10 percent twice a year. In addition, they were commanded to give another 10 percent every three years to provide for the local Levites, aliens, fatherless, and widows.

This would average out to 23 percent of their income each year. This does not include any guilt, sin, or sacrificial giving that's also prescribed by God. In fairness to our current-day situation, it should be noted that these giving levels also covered the social needs of the society, which we pay taxes to cover.

You may be thinking, these are all Old Testament examples, but we're operating under the New Testament now. You may be thinking that because your heart really doesn't want to turn loose of your hard-earned money. If so, I recommend you stick with the Old Testament requirements because they are a lot more stringent than Jesus' requirements.

Jesus clearly wanted us to realize that everything is God's, not just 10 percent, or even 23 percent. He told one rich young ruler to sell all of his possessions and give to the poor in order to enter the kingdom of heaven. He also chastised the Pharisees in Luke 11:42: "Woe to you Pharisees! For you pay tithe of mint and rue and every kind of garden herb, and yet disregard justice and the love of God; but these are the things you should have done without neglecting the others."

The focus throughout the New Testament is on giving generously and recognizing that it all belongs to God. On many occasions, Paul emphasizes generosity and cheerful giving rather than the dogma of the Old Testament teaching on tithing.

> *We need to recognize that God owns it all, including our business profits, and we should hold it all loosely and give when, where, and however much God directs.*

The final point of this survey of Old and New

Testament teaching is that God is looking for us to be generous and cheerful about our giving. We need to recognize that God owns it all, including our business profits, and we should hold it all loosely and give when, where, and however much God directs. Now let's examine the particulars on business giving.

I often hear this question about giving: Do I give from my gross or my net? For businesses, this is often more complicated. The Bible says we are to give the first fruits of our increase. This is referring to the increase in your material possessions. I believe this to be most closely aligned to a company balance sheet rather than the income statement. The balance sheet's primary purpose is to reflect this year's increase in net worth versus previous periods. Net worth increases primarily from *net* profit.

Although I don't mean it to be legalistic, I believe the starting point should be 10 percent of net profit. Over time, God may call you to increase that percentage. I have worked with businesses that believe God has called them to tithe from their gross income. I think if you are called to do that, by all means do it. Not all businesses would be able to do that and stay in business beyond the first year.

For example, a travel agency typically receives less than 10 percent of gross sales as the commission to cover their operating expenses and profit. If they tithed on their gross sales, they would be out of business very quickly. From what I have witnessed in most businesses, any kind of giving to God's work out of business profits would be a great improvement.

Tithing, like many things in life, has become more complicated due to the IRS code. A business today can operate as a sole proprietor, a partnership, a Subchapter S corporation, a C corporation, a Limited Liability Corporation (LLC), a 501(c)(3), or an association. Although these different entities impact the tax consequences, and which entity actually pays the tithe, they don't impact the biblical admonition to give.

If you are tithing from your business surplus and think you have arrived, stop and ask God to search your heart for any idols. Ask him to lead you to the level of giving he desires. If you still have a surplus over your needs and any desires that God has honored, then I am sure somewhere in the kingdom there is someone with a need waiting on your plenty. God may even ask you to donate your entire business to kingdom work, like he did Mr. Tam (in chapter three).

When do you give?

Giving from a business is different than giving from a personal paycheck. When you receive a paycheck, it is usually a set amount every pay period. Using the biblical concept of first fruits, this sort of arrangement would mean that our tithe would come first out of our check on payday.

In biblical times, the business community was primarily made up of farmers. The original concept of tithing related to the farmer's harvest. Since they were to give from their first fruits, it made sense that they had to wait until they had a harvest, which can be different times of the year, depending on the crop or livestock involved.

When a grain harvest was drawing near, there would be a teaser of what was to come. There would be a small amount of harvestable crop, even though it was not yet time for the full harvest. It was from this initial harvest that the concept of first fruits was demonstrated. Farmers would give this beginning harvest to the Lord as an offering to recognize his sovereignty over the entire crop.

There are many sorts of businesses today. Some only have a harvest once or twice a year, but many have some form of harvest each and every day. God's principle has not changed.

He still desires for us to recognize his sovereignty. We should be willing to offer to him our first fruits. The timing is not as critical as your heart's attitude.

How often do you count your harvest? This can be a gauge as to when you should give. If you only monitor your profitability monthly, then monthly is probably a good time for giving. If it's annually, give annually. Naturally, it will need to be when you have cash to give.

Many businesses are seasonal, with months that always show an income loss. It's in those months business owners may wish to have a surplus set aside for cash shortfalls. This may be a valid reason for giving during the months with abundance, but don't hold on to the money too tightly. If God is the provider we have entrusted our life with, he can make the lean months rich if we honor his commands. When you trust God solely and confidently, you may find you no longer have months that lose money.

In Leviticus 19:23–25, the Israelites were commanded not to touch the fruit of the fruit trees for the first three years, then the entire crop for the fourth year was to be holy unto the Lord, so it was the fifth year before there was any harvest that belonged to the farmer.

You can relate to this commandment if you are in the orchard business. It takes a long time for your trees to bear fruit. Pray and ask the Lord about the timing of planting and harvesting for your business. Give your first fruits unto the Lord regularly and consistently.

To whom do we give?

In the book of Leviticus, the Lord clearly designates the Levites as the tribe that was to receive the tithes of their brothers on God's behalf. God actually gifted his tithes to the Levites so they would remember that their inheritance was from God. They were not to share in the division of lands between the tribes. Out of these tithes, the Lord gave the Levites the responsibility for feeding their families and taking care of the repairs and upkeep of the temple and/or places of worship.

Employees. As a business leader, you have responsibility for your "business family." Your first efforts in generosity should be to your own team of people. Some may be dealing with financial situations where they could use some extra help. Although you do not want to enable bad behavior, you do need to consider ways to help when there is an extreme medical or physical need in the family.

Local church. Now that Jesus is our high priest, we no longer follow the ancestral order of the Levites being God's recipients of the tithe. Rather, we follow the principle established of providing for the faithful work of the families of God's full-time servants, and the necessary upkeep of today's places of worship. On another note, if you have a very profitable business, be sensitive to the fact that giving too much to one congregation can sometimes ruin a church. This may be a time to spread it to other ministries.

Para-church ministries. Many of today's ministries recommend that you support your local church with your tithe and give to their ministries only after your first obligation has been met. Although I think this is a good approach, I believe scripture reflects many occasions in Paul's ministry where churches or individuals gave to further Paul's missionary activities, even though he was not necessarily the head of their local church.

Our culture has made ministry complex. During the first century, the church was the vehicle for all ministries. There was not a need to break out separate para-church organizations because the church worked in unity to accomplish all of these purposes. Today in America, we are an independent nation with complex organizational law and tax codes. Due to government social programs, the church has abandoned many of the duties God called us to perform as Christians. Christians have established separate organizations to fill these unmet needs, presenting the business owner/giver with many choices and valid ministries that need funding.

Community and civic needs. Many businesses recognize the need to give back to the community in which they operate their business, even though they might forget to give anything to God's work. Scripture is clear: We are to first give to the needs of our brothers and sisters in Christ, then we are to give to the needs of the poor, widows, and others around us. Choosing how to do this and which organizations to give to can be confusing, and many businesses do a poor job of managing their financial resources in this area.

Boaz is a model of this in the book of Ruth. He complied with God's commands to the Israelites to leave the excess grain from the edges of the fields for the poor in the community. The poor would come onto the land and pick up this excess, which enabled them to share in the harvest of the generous landowner. Businesses today should view this as an example.

People from civic organizations regularly approach businesses for small contributions, often times enticing them with advertising or promotion for their business. Not wanting to offend anyone in the community, they agree to $50 here or $100 there without researching the best choices for these dollars. This is a very reactive—but not effective—approach.

A simple mechanism to help businesses with this issue is to set a budgeted amount for the year. After the budget is set, review the organizations you have been asked to give to in the past and consider other opportunities you feel have been effective and worthwhile in your community. Prioritize this list by considering their impact on the community, and then consider to whom you think God has called you to minister.

Prayerfully consider the impact of each organization, its belief system, and what it promotes to the community. Research its history in regards to how faithful it has been in being good stewards of the resources given to it, as well as whether there might be any negative repercussions to your Christian-run business if it's known you supported this organization. Remember that every dollar spent in this area may have just helped in kingdom work.

Summary

Many owners have never considered that the business they operate has been given to them by God. Therefore, if we truly believe that God is the owner of all things, and he has blessed us with stewarding his business, shouldn't we generously give to others from that business, as he has given to us?

God is a generous God! He desires us to be his ambassadors by being generous to our employees, customers, suppliers, and to our community. We will be blessed if we build our businesses on the solid foundation of God's Word. From that blessing, we can generously give to God's work and experience the abundant joy that flows from that generosity. Do not give out of guilt or compulsion, but learn to give generously and cheerfully.

CHAPTER FOURTEEN
Staying on Track

Remember me for this, my God, and do not blot out what I have so faithfully done for the house of my God and its services.
Nehemiah 13:14

Nehemiah led an amazing project in Jerusalem that resulted in the walls being rebuilt around the city, the city was repopulated, and a spiritual revival broke out. But his work was not done. After he returned to serve the king in Persia, the people of Israel slipped back into their old ways. By the time Nehemiah returned to visit, sin was once again prevalent. Many of the reforms he had implemented were being ignored.

Nehemiah was a passionate man that despised sin. His passion spilled out in an aggressive manor when he learned that many in Israel had returned to marrying women from foreign countries against God's command. We read in Nehemiah 13:25, "I rebuked them and called curses down on them. I beat some of the men and pulled out their hair. I made them take an oath in God's name and said: 'You are not to give your daughters in marriage to their sons, nor are you to take their daughters in marriage for your sons or for yourselves.'"

Nehemiah was willing to hold others accountable. For your business to stay on track with God's plan, you will also need to hold others accountable to the original plan. You can set policies and procedures in place that are in alignment with God, but people are people. They will still disappoint you and turn from God's way and your plan from time to time.

Actually, it's likely that you will go off track at times and need a reminder of God's plan for your business. My desire for this book is that it can become a reference for you. Read it periodically, or review sections of the book to help steer you back on God's path for you and for your business.

God has a plan for you and for your business! He desires you to care for the people whom he has entrusted to you, and to steward well all of the resources that come in and through your business. If you develop a plan with God's input, implement that plan God's way, and lead others accordingly, you will have prepared yourself to receive God's favor and blessing.

It won't always be easy because the enemy desires you to fail, but it will be an exciting adventure that can impact the lives of your family, your team at work, your customers, suppliers, and your entire community.

May God bless you, your family, and your work!

APPENDIX

Business resource list

The following is a list of organizations that may be helpful in your journey of glorifying God in and through your workplace.

Acumen – Helping Business Owners & CEO's Maximize Their Xponential Leadership Impact and Sharpen their Edge by creating instructive, safe, shared-value owner-to-owner affinity-centriq advisory councils that enable iron sharpening iron, wisdom of counsel and vibrant community. www.theacumenedge.com

Alliance Defending Freedom - Works to preserve and defend our most cherished birthright—religious freedom. www.adflegal.org

C12 Group - Helps Christian leaders achieve excellence through best-practice professional development, peer sharpening, consistent accountability, and learning with the eternal perspective in mind. www.c12group.com

CBMC - Encourages individuals to get and stay connected in order to help them grow in their faith. www.cbmc.com

CBMC International - An interdenominational, evangelical Christian organization comprised of national associations around the world. We share a common statement of belief, ministry practices, and a passion to see lives transformed by the Gospel of Jesus Christ. www.cbmcint.com

Center for Faith and Work at LeTourneau University - Helps Christians understand how their work matters to God and his kingdom, and experience Christ's transforming presence and power in every workplace in every nation. www.centerforfaithandwork.com

Convene - Connects, equips and inspires Christian CEOs and business owners to grow exceptional businesses, and become high-impact leaders who honor God. www.convenenow.com

Corporate Chaplains of America - Builds caring relationships with the hope of gaining permission to share the life-changing good news of Jesus Christ in a non-threatening manner. www.chaplain.org

FCCI - Equips and encourages Christian business leaders to operate their businesses and conduct their personal lives in accordance with biblical principles. www.fcci.org

Institute for Faith, Work and Economics – Advances a free and flourishing society by revolutionizing the way people view their work. www.tifwe.org

Liberty Institute - The largest legal organization dedicated solely to defending and restoring religious liberty in America. www.libertyinstitute.org

Lifework Leadership - Transforms leaders so its vision of transforming cities will become a reality. www.lifeworkleadership.org

Made to Flourish - Provides resources, training, events, and local city network gatherings to equip pastors with a deeper understanding of the essential connection between Sunday faith and Monday work. www.madetoflourish.org

Marketplace Leaders - Creates tools that inspire, teach, and connect Christian believers to resources and relationships in order to manifest the life of Christ in their workplace call. www.marketplaceleaders.org

Marketplace Ministries - Shares God's love through chaplains in the workplace by providing personalized and proactive employee care service for client companies. www.marketplaceministries.com

National Christian Foundation - Mobilizes resources by inspiring biblical generosity. www.nationalchristian.com.

National Faith at Work Association - Builds, nurtures, and sustains a broad, inclusive network of Christian ministries, churches, organizations, companies, and individuals in the U.S. dedicated to impacting the workplace and marketplace to the glory of God. www.nfwa.org

NavWorkplace – Encourages others to live out the grace and truth of Jesus where we work through relational communities. www.navworkplace.org

Theology of Work - Helps people explore what the Bible and the Christian faith can contribute to ordinary work. www.theologyofwork.org

Truth at Work – Assists business leaders, entrepreneurs, CEOs, and executives to be the gifted leaders God has created them to be. www.truthatwork.org

Two Ten Magazine - Inspires, encourages, and equips business leaders with Christian principles to make an eternal and positive impact on everyone that God has entrusted them to serve. www.twotenmag.com

Work Matters - Equips men and women to grow in their faith and work journey through major events, workplace small group curriculum, programs, and digital resources. www.workmatters.org

ABOUT RICK BOXX

Rick Boxx, president and CEO of *Integrity Resource Center*, has vast entrepreneurial and business experience. His business experience, coupled with his love of teaching the Bible, has led thousands towards doing business God's way.

Rick's popular "Integrity Moments" broadcast is heard on more than 250 radio stations and delivered by email to more than two million in multiple languages. As a radio personality, author, and speaker, Rick Boxx inspires thousands to put God first in their business and career, and challenges business leaders to live out their faith at work.

As a multiple-time entrepreneur, Bible teacher, former banker, consultant, and CPA, Rick's experience and personal stories will encourage, inspire, and train leaders to honor God in all they do.

Rick is the author of six books and has taught internationally. With more than 20 years of experience, he's known as a pioneer in the faith-at-work movement. He lives in Overland Park, Kansas, with his wife, Kathy, and has three grown children.

INTEGRITY RESOURCE CENTER

Integrity Resource Center is a nonprofit formed in 2001, and dedicated to training and equipping leaders to do business God's way.

Our Vision

One million leaders pleasing God by learning and modeling God's principles in their workplace. (Matthew 5:19) By equipping these leaders to be good stewards of their work, they will be more *purpose driven, courageous, ethical, loving,* and *excellent* in their work. The result will be more leaders who accept Christ and apply their faith and integrity to their work.

Our Mission

To glorify God by helping others learn, model, and teach God's principles in their workplace.

Our Values

Faith – Integrity – Relationships – Excellence

Our hope for one million leaders

Our vision is far more than an organization, programs, or events. *We care about seeing individual lives transformed.* Our strategy is to be the comprehensive resource center that leaders seek out to connect with resources and other organizations that can help them fulfill God's plan for their vocation.

We create awareness for God's plan and purpose for our vocation through radio, events, and speaking engagements. Once awareness is created, we help others learn and model God's principles through providing business counsel, online tools, small group studies, and training and consulting. We teach leaders to train others through our Next Generation Leadership program, our small group leader's kit, and train the trainer programs.

To learn more about how Integrity Resource Center can encourage and equip you for your faith journey in your workplace, visit www.integrityresource.org.

Made in the USA
Charleston, SC
26 January 2017